S0-EQL-736

DIALECTOLOGY: PROBLEMS AND PERSPECTIVES

Edited by
Lorraine Hall Burghardt

Supported by the Better English Fund
established by
JOHN C. HODGES

University of Tennessee ● Knoxville, Tennessee
1971

BELMONT COLLEGE LIBRARY
70565

Contents

Editor's Comments v

Part I: Keynote Address
Comparisons between English and American Word Usage

L.A.N.E. and L.A.E.: Lexical Links 3
    Harold Orton
    Emeritus Professor, University of Leeds, England
    Visiting Professor, University of Tennessee, 1970

Part II: Editorial Approaches to Fieldwork Data

Why Not a Computer as Editor? 41
    Gordon R. Wood
    Professor, Southern Illinois University

Some Problems in Editing the Linguistic Atlas
of the Upper Midwest 54
    Harold B. Allen
    Professor, University of Minnesota

Editorial Problems of an English Linguistic Atlas 79
    Harold Orton
    Emeritus Professor, University of Leeds, England
    Visiting Professor, University of Tennessee, 1970

Part III: Fieldwork in the Southern United States

What Happens in Tennessee? 119
    Raven I. McDavid
    Professor, University of Chicago

Southern Speech and the LAGS Project 130
    Lee Pederson
    Professor, Emory University

Editor's Comments

During the winter and spring of 1970, Professor Harold Orton was a visiting professor on the Knoxville campus of the University of Tennessee. He brought with him from England a vast knowledge about our language and an unbounded enthusiasm for his work. With this as an impetus, it was decided that a two-day conference would be held where an exchange of ideas and information could take place. On April 17–18, 1970, in honor of the 175th anniversary of the University of Tennessee, a conference on Dialectology: Problems and Perspectives was held. This book is a recording of those proceedings.

The featured speaker was Harold Orton, professor emeritus of Leeds University, England. Professor Orton began his work on dialects with a 1933 book, *The Phonology of a South Durham Dialect,* on the speech of his own village. His *Survey of English Dialects,* with an *Introduction* and ten volumes already published and two more in press, is one of the most comprehensive studies of its type. He is honorary editor-in-chief of this series, which includes a *Linguistic Atlas of England,* now in preparation. It contains the results of an eleven-year field survey initiated by the late Professor Eugen Dieth of Zurich and Professor Orton himself. Professor Orton has published numerous articles on English regional dialect and he is also the co-author, with the late Professor W. L. Renwick, of *The Beginnings of English Literature to Skelton 1509.* Together with Professor Nathalia Wright, he is preparing a *Word Geography of England* for early publication.

A group of outstanding American dialectologists also participated in the conference. Professor Harold Allen, of the University of Minnesota, is the director of the *Linguistic Atlas of the Upper Midwest.* He has also edited *Readings in Applied English Linguistics* and the *Bibliography of American Linguistics.* He has published numerous articles on dialect differences.

Professor Gordon Wood of the Southern Illinois University, Edwardsville campus, is especially interested in the distribution of vocabulary in the states of the Mississippi Valley. He has published articles on this topic in *Publications of the American Dialect Society*. He has authored *Sub-Regional Speech Variations in Vocabulary, Grammar, and Pronunciation*, a research project sponsored by the Office of Education, and *Vocabulary Change: A Study of Variation in Regional Words of Eight of the Southern States*.

Professor Raven I. McDavid of the University of Chicago, who has spent thousands of hours as a field investigator for the Linguistic Atlas of the United States and Canada, has published more than 150 technical reviews and articles. He is interested in the relationship between dialect differences and their social causes. He is the author of a chapter on American dialects in *The Structure of American English* by W. Nelson Francis, *The Pronunciation of English in the Atlantic States* with Hans Kurath, and the abridgement of H. L. Mencken's *The American Language*.

Professor Lee Pederson of Emory University is a former student of Raven McDavid. He is the author of an intensive study of Chicago speech and many articles on southern speech. Currently, he is the director of the Linguistic Atlas of the Gulf States, a project which is in the process of recording the speech differences of many states which have been previously ignored.

The format of the conference was so designed that three major areas served as the focus for the discussion. The keynote address by Orton placed dialectology on a broader scale, so to speak, by discussing the comparisons and contrasts between words in England and in America. The second aspect of the conference was devoted to the problems entailed in tabulating, recording, and analysing the data collected from linguistic field records. Professors Orton, Wood, and Allen presented three approaches for dealing with these problems. The third and final aspect discussed the work now being done on the Gulf States and the interior south. The talks by Professors McDavid and Pederson were addressed toward this.

This conference was made possible through the generosity of the English department and funds from the Better English Fund, established by the late John C. Hodges, who was head of that department for many years. I am indebted to Kenneth L. Knickerbocker, head of the department at that time and now vice-president for academic affairs, for his suggestions. Professor Nathalia Wright has also so very generously donated her time to this project.

Lorraine Hall Burghardt
Knoxville, Tennessee
February 1971

Part I: Keynote Address
Comparisons between English and American Word Usage

L.A.N.E. AND L.A.E.: LEXICAL LINKS

Harold Orton

Emeritus Professor, University of Leeds, England
Visiting Professor, University of Tennessee, 1970

With so many distinguished American dialectologists in the audience, this is for me a formidable occasion. But I am delighted to see several old friends again, and I look forward to making many new ones during the Conference and, of course, to hearing about their own dialect-hunting in various parts of the U.S. I shall miss, however, your Nelson Francis in particular, for he was one of the nine fieldworkers in our English Dialect Survey. He carried out his task with great relish and enthusiasm and made an excellent contribution of twelve field-recordings to the 313 in our archives.

My theme this evening has obviously wide and deep ramifications, and I am quite ill-prepared to do the subject justice. Again, the title of my talk is as rash as it is misleading. What I had in mind when choosing it was to use the occasion for, firstly, reporting briefly upon a survey of dialectal English in England that has occupied so much of my time between 1946 and now; secondly, for showing you some of its results on slides and thereby calling attention to a few parallel usages in the English spoken on both sides of the Atlantic; and, thirdly, for playing to you two or three samples of traditional regional English dialect that is now fast disappearing. However, my title would restrict my search for American correspondences simply to the six New England States of L.A.N.E. Yet with W.G.E.U.S. also available, namely Hans Kurath's admirable *World Geography of the Eastern United States* (1949), the researcher has access to information from all the States on the Atlantic Seaboard. Something, therefore, would be lost to me this evening by not taking my comparisons from both L.A.N.E. and W.G.E.U.S. So when stepping beyond L.A.N.E. into W.G.E.U.S., you will perhaps be kind enough to indulge me.

The first results of our English Dialect Survey are now appearing in the series *Survey of English Dialects*,[1] founded in 1962. Yet the fact that only ten of the twelve books of Basic Material have so far been published—two arrived here only yesterday—has in effect limited my search for comparable information to virtually only the first third of the material. So my talk will seem to you rather sketchy, especially when contrasted with Nelson Francis' short paper entitled "Some Dialect lsoglosses in England" printed in *American Speech* of December 1959. This illuminating paper was actually the first attempt made by anyone to compare the results of the English Dialect Survey itself—then still incomplete—with those of the great American Survey of the thirties and forties as reported in L.A.N.E. and W.G.E.U.S.

Not unnaturally, many people look for regional usages common to both American and British English. The search will doubtless become more rewarding when all the British material recently collected in both England and Scotland appears in print. But there is a far wider question—so clearly posed by Nelson Francis—of identifying "the complex patterns established by the wholesale transfer of the English language from the Old World to the New." The investigation of this enormous problem is likely to start soon. The publication of various linguistic atlases, e.g., by my distinguished colleagues who will be speaking tomorrow morning, and of Cassidy's eagerly awaited *Dictionary of American Regional English*, should certainly ensure its success. Meanwhile, Francis, with access only to limited information from English dialects, demonstrated four, possibly five different kinds of relationships in the five lexical examples he dealt with, namely the notions GUTTER, RIVULET, SWINGLETREE, PET LAMB, and AFTERMATH.

Since so many of you are much more competent than I to speak about L.A.N.E. and W.G.E.U.S., I shall be brief in my remarks about them. Both are based on the results of separate surveys of the regions concerned but are carried out under the direction of

---

[1]Ed. Harold Orton and Eugen Dieth.† (Leeds: E. J. Arnold and Son [publ. for the University of Leeds], 1962–   ). All the books comprising the first stage of this series, thirteen volumes (the *Introduction* and twelve books of Basic Material), are now published. H.O., Oct. 1, 1971.

that great man, Hans Kurath. The New England States were investigated between 1931 and 1933; and the Middle and South Atlantic States between 1933 and 1949—the Second World War had considerably interrupted the programme. Both surveys formed part of a larger plan, drawn up in 1930 and sponsored by the American Council of Learned Societies, for the systematic investigation of all the varieties of English spoken in the U.S. and Canada. The plan also embraced several closely related but quite autonomous projects. These are now in progress in other parts of this vast region. We shall be learning tomorrow morning about some of these projects from the directors themselves. The survey in the States of the Eastern Seaboard has led to the production, among other publications, of both L.A.N.E. and W.G.E.U.S. The first of these linguistic atlases, L.A.N.E., edited by Kurath and others and published between 1939 and 1943, comprises 734 beautifully executed, factual and non-interpretive, large-sized maps, issued in six massive books. On the maps are printed the phonetic transcriptions of local speech usages obtained by fieldworkers using a comprehensive notional questionnaire of between 800 and 850 questions about pronunciation, grammar, and vocabulary. Raven McDavid, the present custodian of the archives in the University of Chicago where they had been transferred from the University of Michigan at Ann Arbor after Kurath's retirement, has been most closely associated throughout with these monumental Surveys, first as a fieldworker in the East and later as co-author with Kurath of the *Pronunciation of English in the Atlantic States* (1961).

The second source book, the *Word Geography of the Eastern United States*, edited by Kurath and first published in 1949, succinctly describes the speech areas of the Eastern States, summarily discusses the regional and local words found in this region, and prints 163 simply drawn figures or maps showing the distribution of the synonyms for some of the notions collected during the field survey. These achievements—and others that could well be mentioned here—form a striking tribute to American enterprise and organisation, and at the same time must provide tremendous encouragement and stimulation to American philologists working, or thinking of working, in this field of study.

It is time to turn to the Leeds L.A.E., an abbreviation that at present stands for something actually non-existent. By comparison, L.A.E. has had quite small beginnings. The original project, which aimed at the compilation of a linguistic atlas of England (and of Scotland too), was started quite privately by two men working in the closest collaboration, namely my old friend Eugen Dieth of Zurich and myself. A reasonably full account of this project was published in 1962 in my *Introduction* to the *Survey of English Dialects*.[2] Very briefly, the project was first planned in 1946; the *Questionnaire*, specially compiled by Dieth and me, was first printed in its fifth version in 1952, the fieldwork lasted from 1950 to 1961, and the series of twelve books of Basic Material, designed to contain some of the results of the survey, began to appear in 1962. The last two of these books, now going through the press, will complete the first stage of our publication programme. On my return home in June, I start, together with a new collaborator, on L.A.E. My original collaborator, Eugen Dieth, alas, died unexpectedly in 1956. But long before his untimely death, the project was being wholly carried out from my Department of English Language in the University of Leeds. Fortunately for us, the University of Leeds, from 1964 onwards—the year of my retirement from my chair in the University—arranged to finance a five-year editorial and publishing programme. This followed upon the University-assisted programme that enabled us to issue the *Introduction* and the 3 Parts of Volume I of the Basic Material in 1962-3. The Five-Year Plan came to an end last September, with the programme concerned not then complete, but almost so. My colleagues and I are inexpressibly grateful to the University of Leeds for its great generosity in providing almost all the supporting finance apart from grants from educational trusts and private donors, and more recently from six annual grants of £1000 from the British Academy. Yet subventions, as with our American counterparts, have never been easy to come by.

[At this point the speaker played three tape-recordings of certain elderly, dialect-speaking native informants, who were interviewed during the survey at localities in Somerset, Warwickshire and Yorkshire West Riding.]

Now for a few facts about the English Dialect Survey. Will you

---

[2] Pp. 14–20.

please look at the sample page of the *Questionnaire* that has been circulated [see Fig. 1 below]. The *Questionnaire* that we used, of which you have one whole page in your hands, contains over 1300 unnumbered questions. All the questions were drawn up in full. We wanted to insure that we obtained fully comparable responses. The fieldworkers were briefed to ask all the questions as formu-

QUESTIONNAIRE   49

THE FARM   BOOK I

1   THE FARMSTEAD

Show an aerial photograph of a farmstead and surrounding fields ☐.

1 ... these? **Fields.**
2 ... this? **Farmstead.**
3 ... this? **Farmyard.**
4 ... this? **Stackyard.**
    ... the various buildings?

If necessary, ask the relevant question below.

5 ... the place where you keep pigs? **Pigsty.**—April 1953, *the animals that go (i. grunting)* replaced *pigs*.
6 ... the place where you keep hens? **Hen-house.**—April 1953, *the birds that lay eggs for you* replaced *hens*.
7 ... the place where you keep pigeons? **Dove-cote.**—April 1953, *the birds that go (i. cooing)* replaced *pigeons*.
8 ... the place where you keep your cows? **Cow-house.**—April 1953, *the animals that give you milk* replaced *your cows*.
9 ... the yard in which cattle are kept, especially during the winter, for fattening, and for producing dung? **Straw-yard.**
    Verify the kind of cattle and the purpose.
10 ... the small enclosed piece of pasture near the farmhouse, the place where you might put a cow or a pony that's none too well? **Paddock.**
11 Rev. What's the **barn** for and where is it?

2   THE WORKMEN ON THE FARM

Ask what men work on the farm and what each does. If he omits any of the following notions, ask the relevant questions below.

1 ... the man who looks after those animals that give us wool? **Shepherd.**
2 ... the man in charge of the vehicles? **Cartman.**
3 ... the man who looks after the cows? **Cowman.**—April 1953, *animals that give you milk* replaced *cows*.
4 ... the man who is put on to any task and does general work on a farm? **Farm-labourer.**—April 1953, *sort of task* replaced *task and does general work*.

3   THE COW-HOUSE

Show a picture of an old-fashioned cow-house ☐.

1 ... this? **Stall.**
2 ... this, between the stalls? **Partition.**
3 ... this, for tethering? **Tethering-stake.**

Fig. 1

lated. Such a linguistic questionnaire, with questions set out in detail, was at the time, and so far as I know, a novelty.

We used nine fully trained fieldworkers to apply the *Questionnaire* and they transcribed the informants' responses impressionistically in the alphabet of the International Phonetic Association. Two of the fieldworkers were American, one being Nelson Francis, as mentioned above. Five of the nine had previously written their own theses on English dialects in my Department for Leeds University degrees. All of the fieldworkers were carefully trained to the same pattern and often checked their phonetic notions with the I.P.A. gramophone records of cardinal vowel sounds.

The informants were usually men or women of sixty or more. All were specially chosen by the fieldworkers themselves after enquiries on the spot. In order to save time and money, the field workers were authorised to use more than one informant according to their own judgment. The informants gave their services quite voluntarily. The localities were selected in advance according to geographical position, population figures, and their degree of rurality.

[Here the speaker showed several slides illustrating various aspects of the field-recording.]

In conclusion I shall show you a number of maps on slides depicting certain English speech-usages with counterparts in the States on the Atlantic Seaboard, and I shall explain, from information contained in L.A.N.E. and W.G.E.U.S., where these equivalents occur.

[For a full explanation of the methods and procedures used in preparing the maps below, see pp. 79-84. The following abbreviations are used in the Notes on the maps: excl(uding), Fig(ure), freq(uently), fr(om), gen(eral), M(ap), occ(asionally), rec(orded), ref(erring), reg(ular), spor(adically), usu(ally).]

Postscript.

For initially typing the legends, the labels, and the notes on the maps in both of my papers in this volume, I am indebted to Miss Lynn Acuff of the clerical staff of the Department of English, University of Tennessee.

To my Departmental colleague, Dr. Nathalia Wright, I am specially grateful for considerable help in preparing all my maps in this volume and for many penetrating questions about their format in draft and the information they contain. Her help has been invaluable.

H. O.

LINGUISTIC ATLAS OF ENGLAND

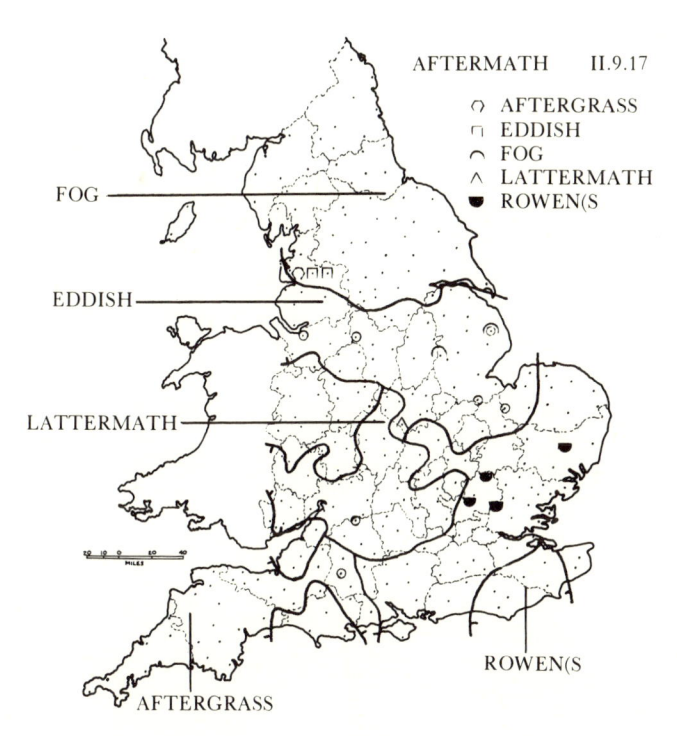

AFTERMATH   II.9.17

○ AFTERGRASS
⊓ EDDISH
⌒ FOG
∧ LATTERMATH
● ROWEN(S

FOG

EDDISH

LATTERMATH

ROWEN(S

AFTERGRASS

Note. ROWAN rec. New England excl. Maine, New York State & occ. Ohio (Western Reserve); and AFTERGRASS spor. fr. New Brunswick to Lake Erie, W.G.E.U.S., pp. 16, 67 & Fig. 112. Cf. L.A.N.E., M. 125.

FIG. 2

LINGUISTIC ATLAS OF ENGLAND

AFTERMATH   II.9.17

○ SECOND CROP

SECOND CUT

SECOND CROP

SECOND CROP

SECOND CUT

SECOND CROP

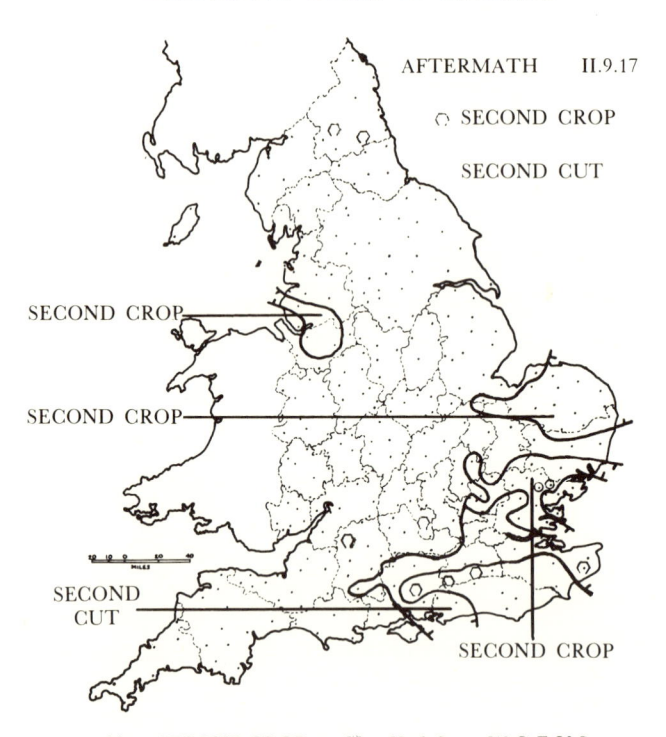

Note. SECOND CROP rec. New York State, W.G.E.U.S., p. 16. SECOND CUTTING very rarely rec. New England, cf. L.A.N.E., M. 125

Fig. 3

LINGUISTIC ATLAS OF ENGLAND

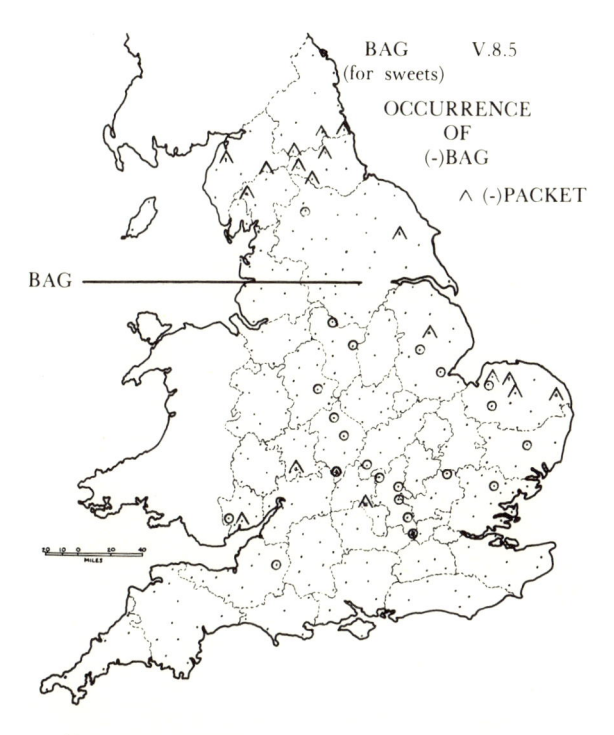

BAG V.8.5
(for sweets)

OCCURRENCE
OF
(-)BAG

∧ (-)PACKET

BAG ―――――

Note. PAPER-BAG "widely current in Eastern States," W.G.E.U.S., p. 56 & Fig. 70. Note also POKE on Fig. 21 below.

Fig. 4

12   Dialectology: Problems and Perspectives

LINGUISTIC ATLAS OF ENGLAND

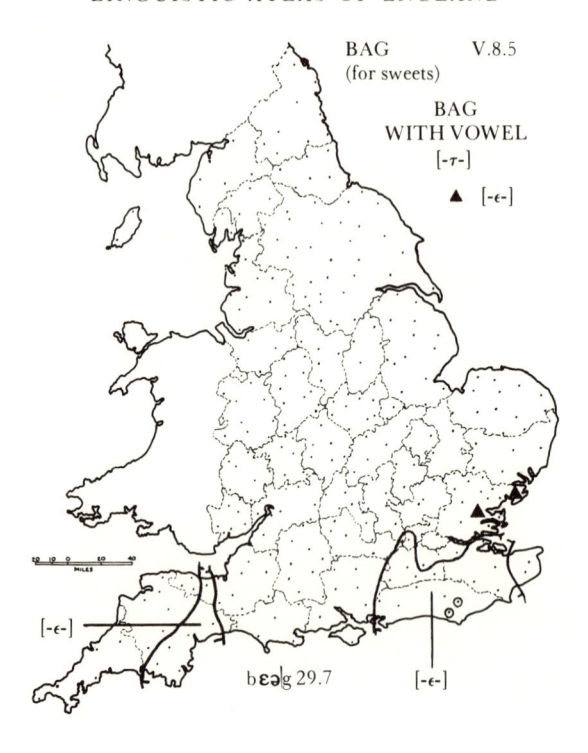

BAG   V.8.5
(for sweets)

BAG
WITH VOWEL
[-ʏ-]
▲   [-ɛ-]

[-ɛ-]

bɛəg 29.7   [-ɛ-]

Fig. 5

LINGUISTIC ATLAS OF ENGLAND

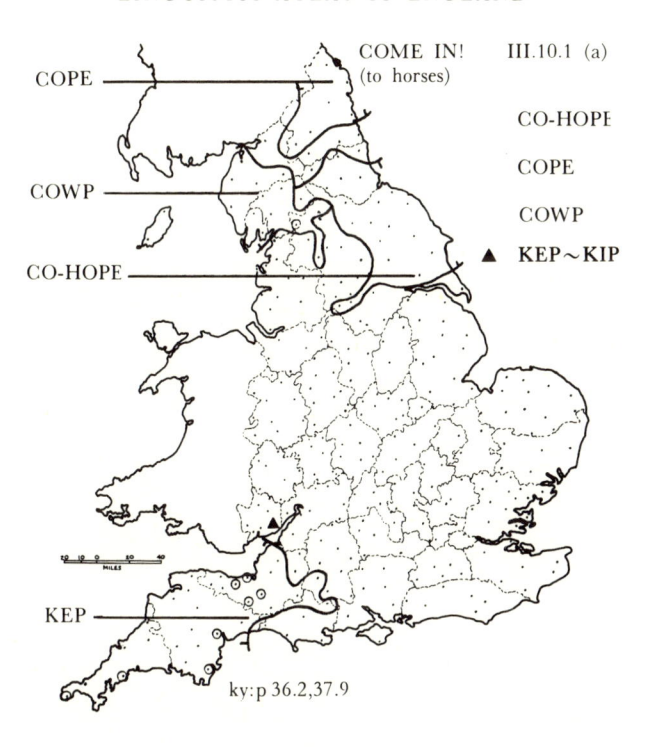

COPE

COME IN! III.10.1 (a)
(to horses)

CO-HOPE

COPE

COWP

COWP

▲ KEP~KIP

CO-HOPE

KEP

ky:p 36.2, 37.9

Fig. 6

LINGUISTIC ATLAS OF ENGLAND

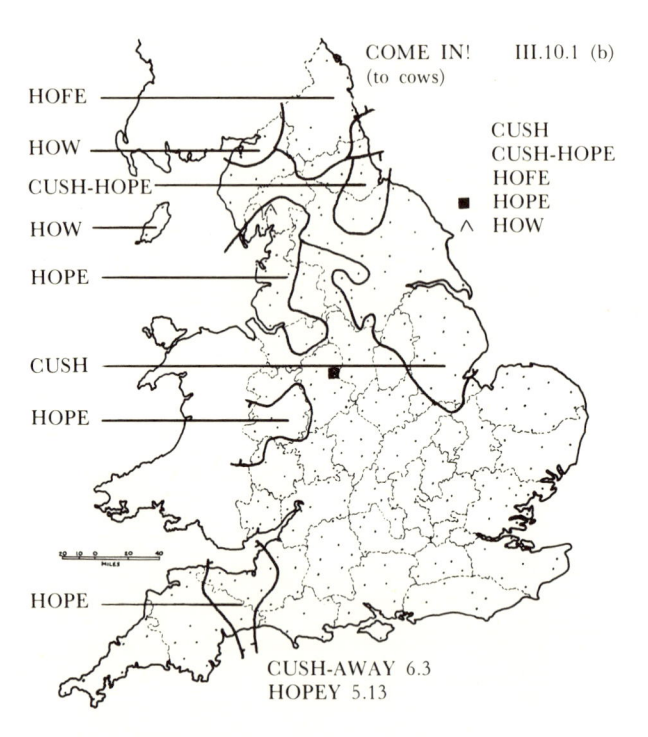

COME IN! III.10.1 (b)
(to cows)

HOFE
HOW
CUSH-HOPE
HOW
HOPE

CUSH
CUSH-HOPE
HOFE
HOPE
HOW

CUSH
HOPE

HOPE

CUSH-AWAY 6.3
HOPEY 5.13

Note. CUSH(IE) rec. northern New Jersey, spor. in Delaware & in Hudson Valley, W.G.E.U.S., p. 63 & Fig. 100.

Fig. 7

LINGUISTIC ATLAS OF ENGLAND

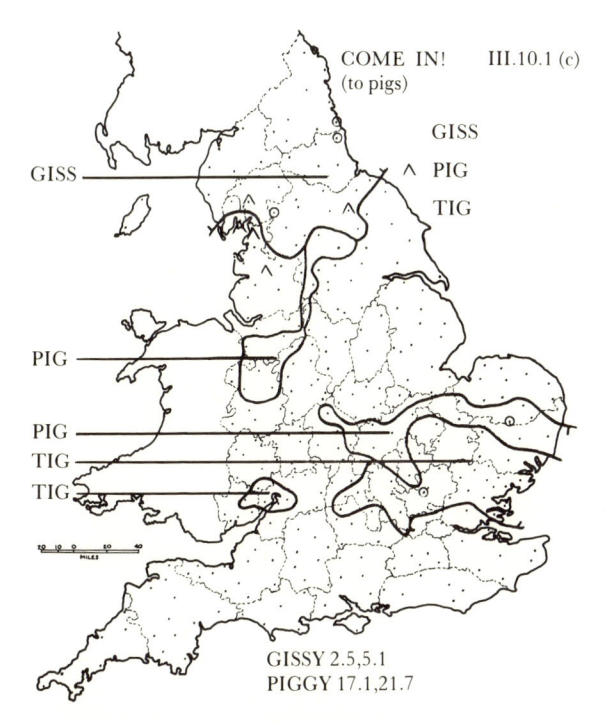

COME IN! III.10.1 (c)
(to pigs)

GISS
GISS
PIG
TIG

PIG

PIG
TIG
TIG

GISSY 2.5, 5.1
PIGGY 17.1, 21.7

Note. PIG(GIE) rec. throughout New England & "Midland areas" excl. Pennsylvania German settlements, W.G.E.U.S., pp. 64–65 & Fig. 104.

Fig. 8

Dialectology: Problems and Perspectives

LINGUISTIC ATLAS OF ENGLAND

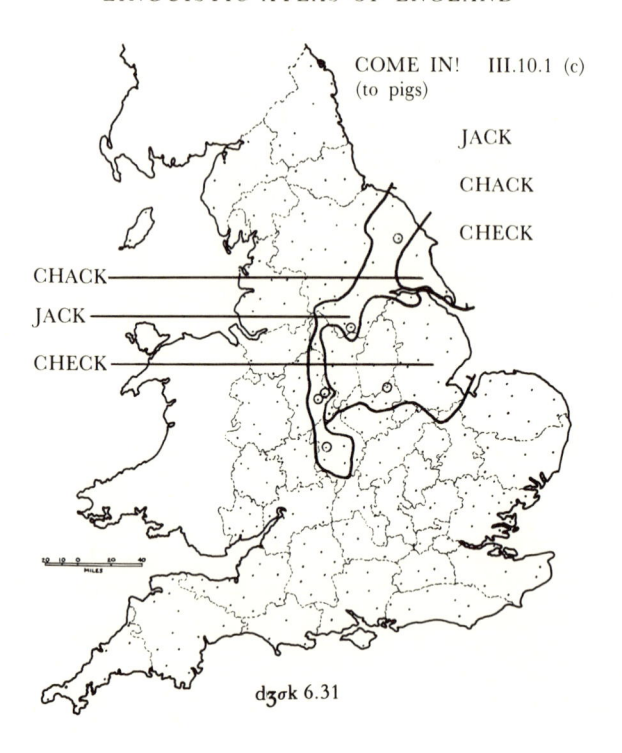

COME IN! III.10.1 (c)
(to pigs)

JACK
CHACK
CHECK

CHACK
JACK
CHECK

dʒσk 6.31

Fig. 9

LINGUISTIC ATLAS OF ENGLAND

COWHOUSE I.1.8

■ COWHOUSE
∧ COW-STABLE

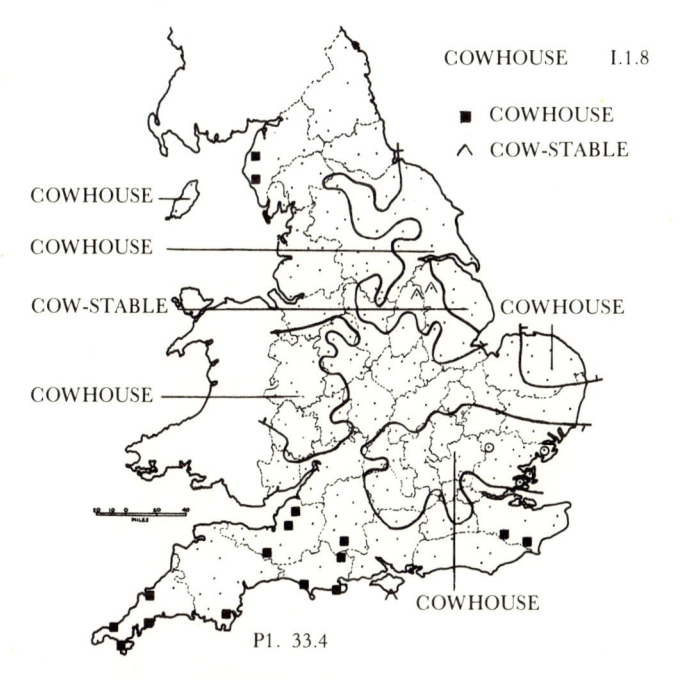

COWHOUSE
COWHOUSE
COW-STABLE
COWHOUSE
COWHOUSE
COWHOUSE
Pl. 33.4

Note. COWHOUSE characteristic of central Virginia Piedmont, W.G.E.U.S., Fig. 31. COWSTABLE occurs spor. in Eastern States, cf. L.A.N.E., M. 108.

Fig. 10

LINGUISTIC ATLAS OF ENGLAND

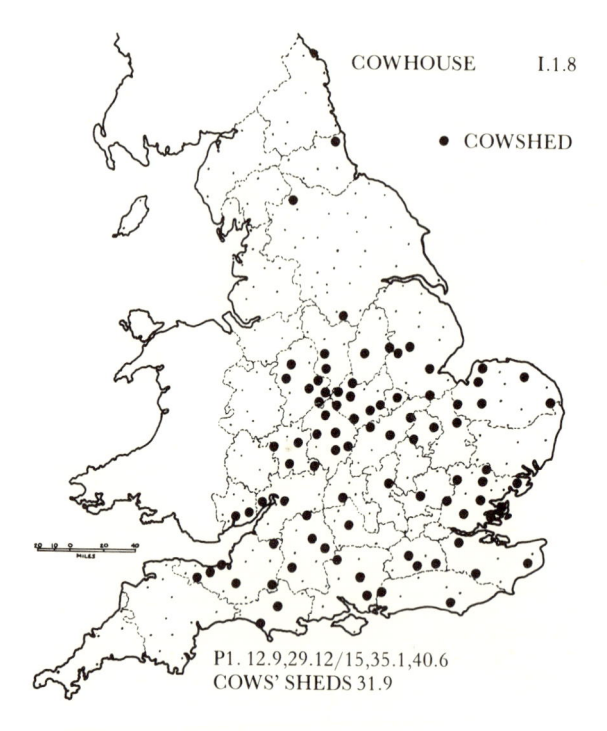

COWHOUSE   I.1.8

• COWSHED

Pl. 12.9, 29.12/15, 35.1, 40.6
COWS' SHEDS 31.9

Note. COWSHED used in New England of a small addition to the barn, cf. L.A.N.E., M. 108.

Fig. 11

LINGUISTIC ATLAS OF ENGLAND

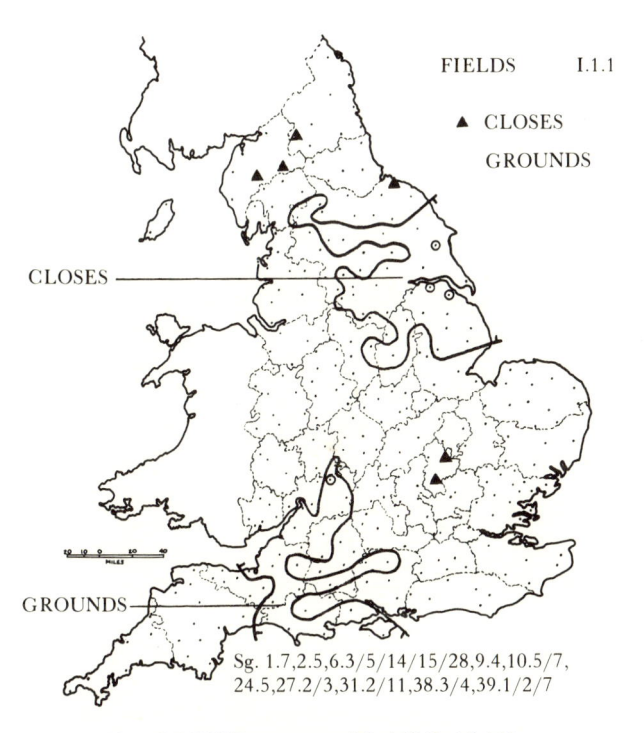

FIELDS   I.1.1

▲ CLOSES
  GROUNDS

CLOSES

GROUNDS

Sg. 1.7,2.5,6.3/5/14/15/28,9.4,10.5/7,
24.5,27.2/3,31.2/11,38.3/4,39.1/2/7

Note. GROUND very rare, cf. L.A.N.E., M. 120.

Fig. 12

LINGUISTIC ATLAS OF ENGLAND

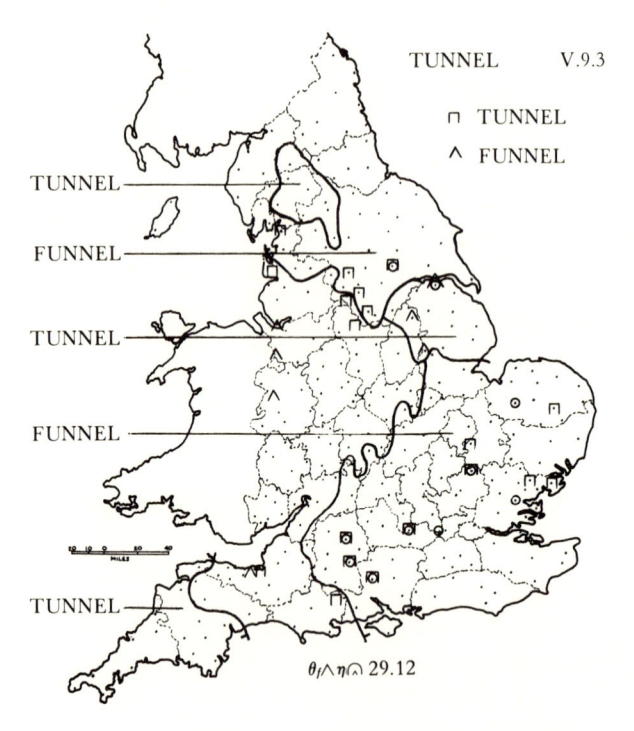

TUNNEL V.9.3

⊓ TUNNEL
∧ FUNNEL

TUNNEL
FUNNEL
TUNNEL
FUNNEL
TUNNEL

$\theta_f \wedge \eta_{\cap}$ 29.12

Note. FUNNEL rec. Hudson Valley & widely in southern New England; TUNNEL rec. New England & Upstate New York though "not common" here, W.G.E.U.S., p. 116. See also L.A.N.E., M. 145.

Fig. 13

LINGUISTIC ATLAS OF ENGLAND

NEAR-HORSE   I.6.4
(ref. wagon-horses)

NEAR(-HORSE)

NEAR-HORSE
NEAR-SIDE(-HORSE)

NEAR(-HORSE)

NEAR(-HORSE)

NEAR(-HORSE)

NEAR(-HORSE)

NEAR(-HORSE)   NEAR(-HORSE)

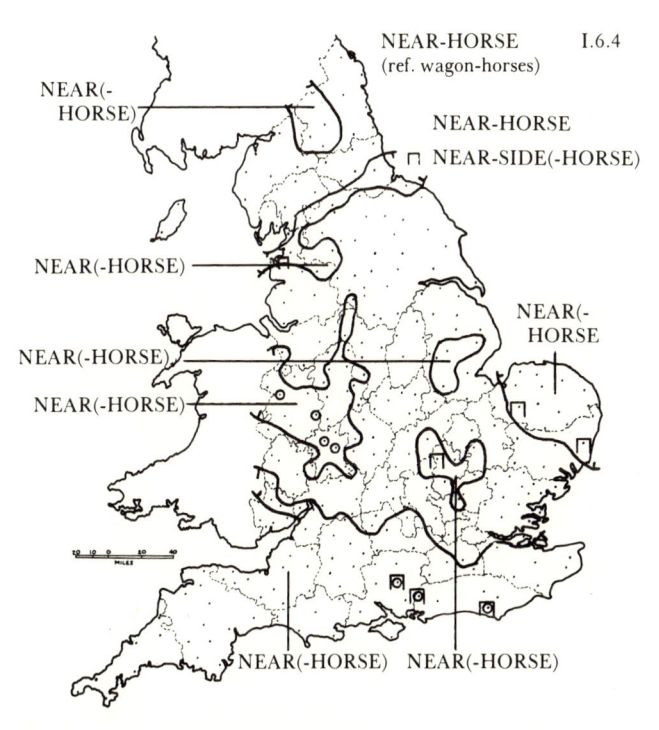

Note. NEAR-HORSE (ref. one of a team) rec. freq. fr. Connecticut River to Potomac, excl. s.w. Pennsylvania, W.G.E.U.S., Fig. 170.

Fig. 14

LINGUISTIC ATLAS OF ENGLAND

NEAR-HORSE I.6.4
(ref. wagon-horses)

NEAR-SIDE(-HORSE)
◯ NEAR-HORSE

NEAR-SIDE(-HORSE)

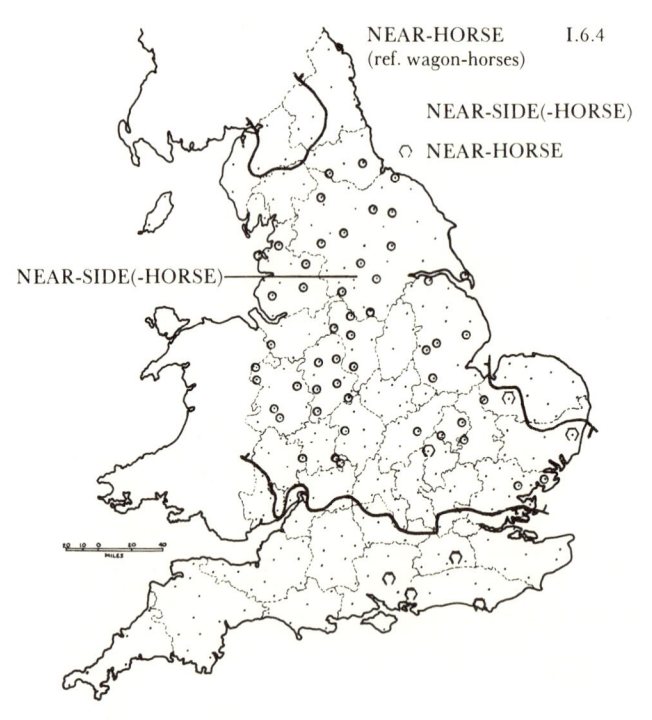

Note. NEAR-SIDE-HORSE rec. Virginia & southern–central Pennsylvania, W.G.E.U.S., Fig. 109.

Fig. 15

LINGUISTIC ATLAS OF ENGLAND

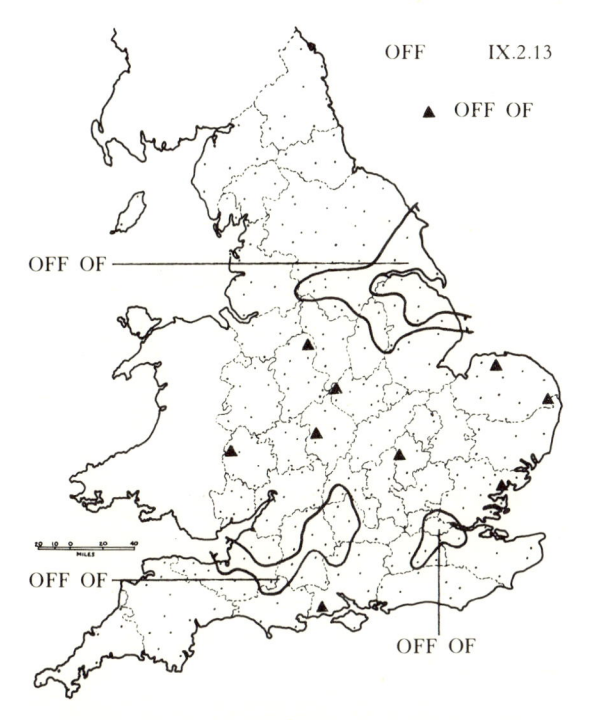

OFF IX.2.13

▲ OFF OF

OFF OF

OFF OF

OFF OF

Note. OFF OF rec. freq. New England, L.A.N.E., M. 724. Freq. heard in Tennessee.

Fig. 16

LINGUISTIC ATLAS OF ENGLAND

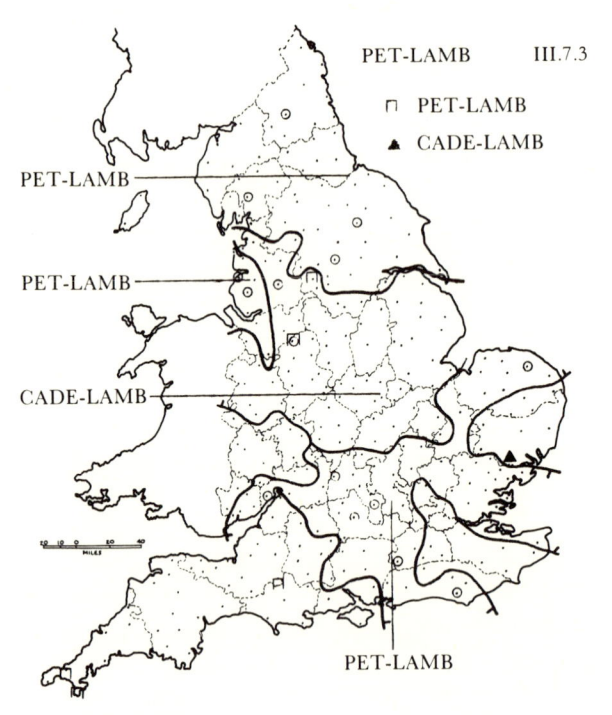

Note. CADE-LAMB rec. fr. Narragansett Bay to Cape Cod, W.G.E.U.S., Fig. 112. Cf. also W.N. Francis, "Some Dialect Isoglosses," *Amer. Speech*, Dec. 1959.

Fig. 17

LINGUISTIC ATLAS OF ENGLAND

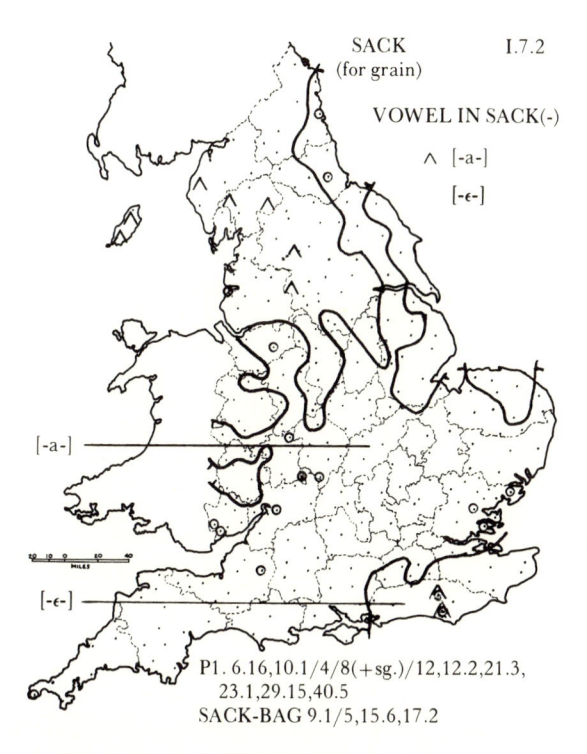

SACK I.7.2
(for grain)

VOWEL IN SACK(-)

∧ [-a-]

[-ɛ-]

[-a-]

[-ɛ-]

Pl. 6.16,10.1/4/8(+sg.)/12,12.2,21.3,
23.1,29.15,40.5
SACK-BAG 9.1/5,15.6,17.2

Note. BURLAP SACK in this sense is in reg. use in the Eastern States, W.G.E.U.S., p. 55.

Fig. 18

26   Dialectology: Problems and Perspectives

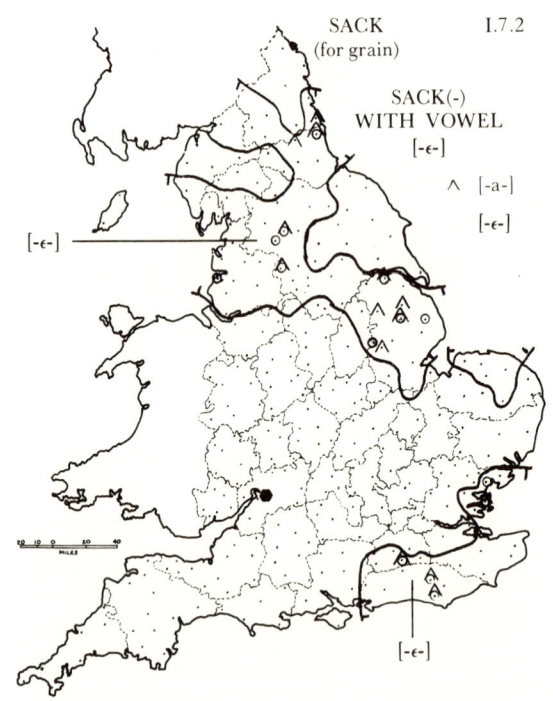

LINGUISTIC ATLAS OF ENGLAND

SACK   I.7.2
(for grain)

SACK(-)
WITH VOWEL
[-ϵ-]

∧ [-a-]

[-ϵ-]

[-ϵ-]

[-ϵ-]

Note. The Northern form with [-ϵ-] represents ON *sekkr*, while the southeastern form corresponds to OE *sacc*.

Fig. 19

LINGUISTIC ATLAS OF ENGLAND

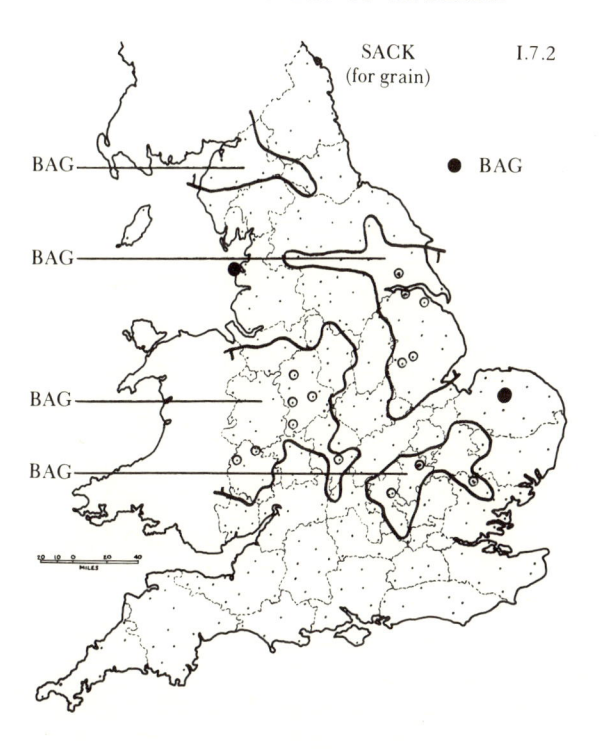

SACK (for grain) I.7.2

Fig. 20

LINGUISTIC ATLAS OF ENGLAND

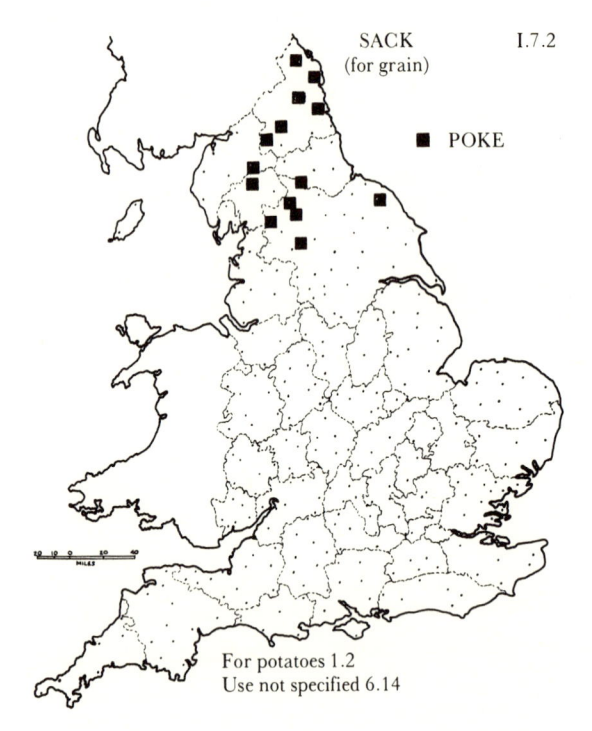

SACK I.7.2
(for grain)

■ POKE

For potatoes 1.2
Use not specified 6.14

Note. POKE meaning, however, "paper-bag" is in gen. use in western Atlantic States, fr. Pennsylvania into northern South Carolina, cf. W.G.E.U.S., Fig. 70.

Fig. 21

LINGUISTIC ATLAS OF ENGLAND

SPRING ONIONS V.7.16

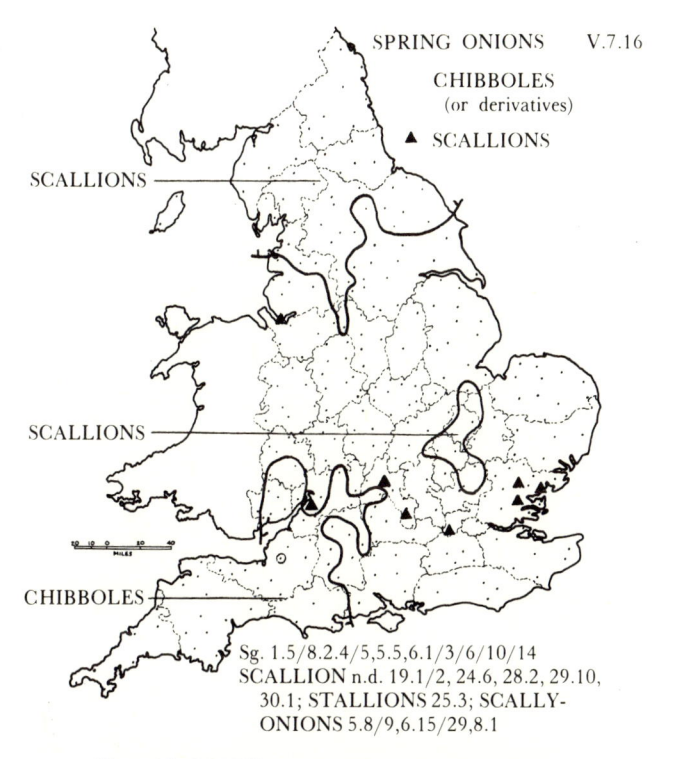

CHIBBOLES (or derivatives)

▲ SCALLIONS

SCALLIONS

SCALLIONS

CHIBBOLES

Sg. 1.5/8.2.4/5,5.5,6.1/3/6/10/14 SCALLION n.d. 19.1/2, 24.6, 28.2, 29.10, 30.1; STALLIONS 25.3; SCALLY-ONIONS 5.8/9,6.15/29,8.1

Note. SCALLION occurs "all parts of New England," L.A.N.E., M. 258. Also in Tennessee. CHIBBOLE rec. only at locality 304.2 (viz. Rye, Rockingham Co., N.H.), L.A.N.E., M. 258.

Fig. 22

LINGUISTIC ATLAS OF ENGLAND

SPRING ONIONS V.7.16

◠ SPRING ONIONS
∧ GREEN ONIONS

SPRING ONIONS
GREEN ONIONS
GREEN ON-
IONS
SPRING ONIONS
SPRING ONIONS

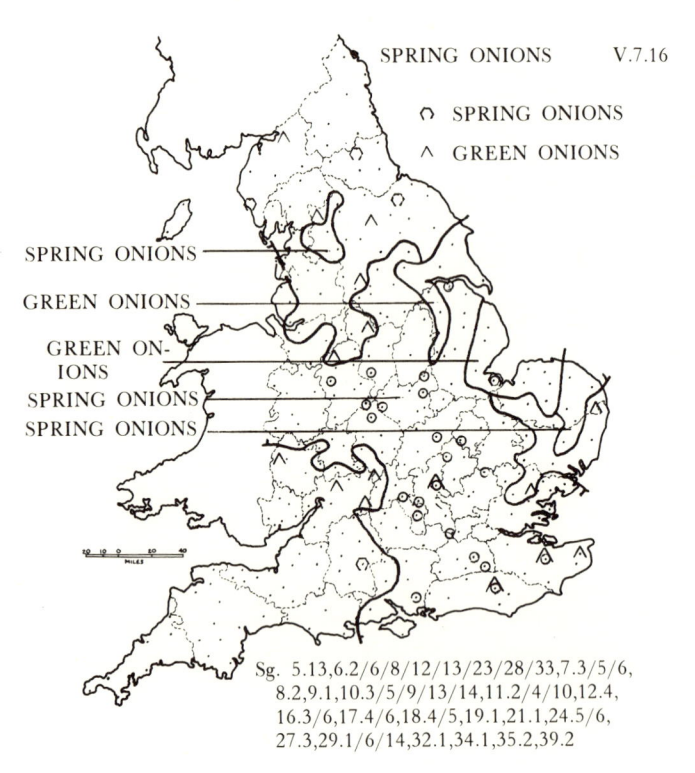

Sg. 5.13,6.2/6/8/12/13/23/28/33,7.3/5/6,
8.2,9.1,10.3/5/9/13/14,11.2/4/10,12.4,
16.3/6,17.4/6,18.4/5,19.1,21.1,24.5/6,
27.3,29.1/6/14,32.1,34.1,35.2,39.2

Note. SPRING ONIONS quite rare in New England,
cf. L.A.N.E., M. 258.

Fig. 23

LINGUISTIC ATLAS OF ENGLAND

SPRING ONIONS   V. 7.16
▲ YOUNG ONIONS
□ SHALLOTS

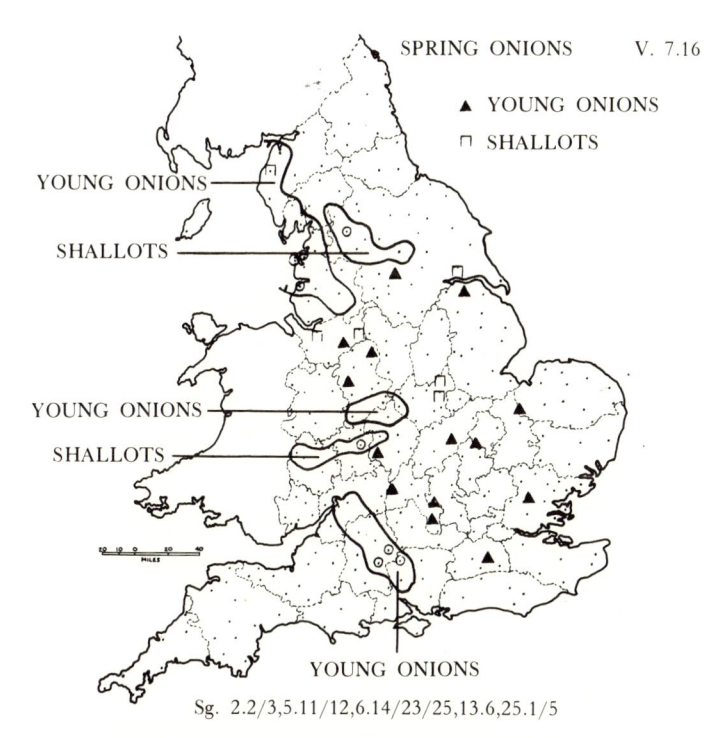

YOUNG ONIONS
SHALLOTS
YOUNG ONIONS
SHALLOTS
YOUNG ONIONS

Sg. 2.2/3, 5.11/12, 6.14/23/25, 13.6, 25.1/5

Note. SHALLOTS and YOUNG ONIONS rarely rec. New England, cf. L.A.N.E., M. 258.

Fig. 24

LINGUISTIC ATLAS OF ENGLAND

SPRING ONIONS   V.7.16

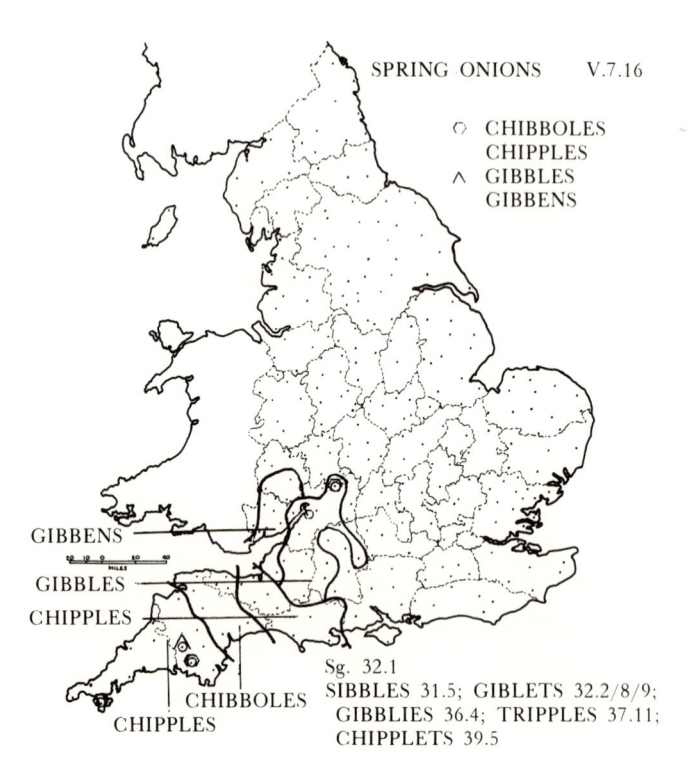

○ CHIBBOLES
  CHIPPLES
∧ GIBBLES
  GIBBENS

GIBBENS
GIBBLES
CHIPPLES

CHIBBOLES
CHIPPLES

Sg. 32.1
SIBBLES 31.5; GIBLETS 32.2/8/9;
GIBBLIES 36.4; TRIPPLES 37.11;
CHIPPLETS 39.5

Fig. 25

LINGUISTIC ATLAS OF ENGLAND

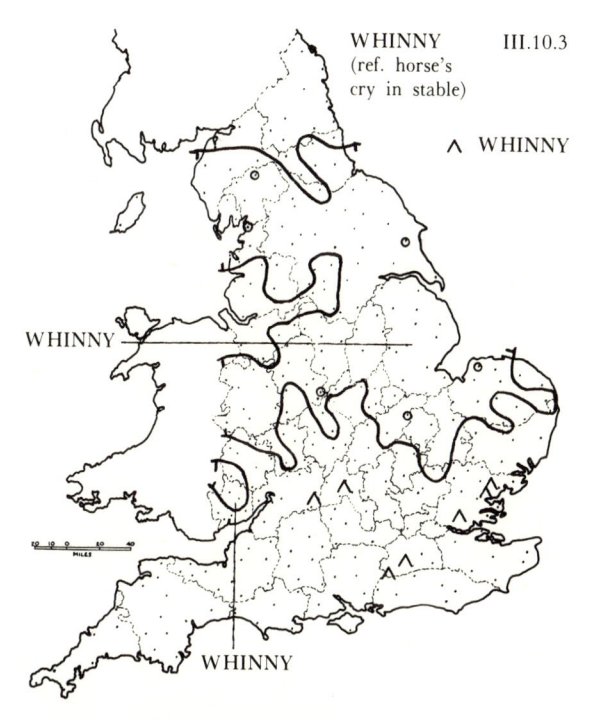

WHINNY III.10.3
(ref. horse's cry in stable)

∧ WHINNY

WHINNY

WHINNY

Note. WHINNY commonly rec. New England, W.G.E.U.S., pp. 62–63 & Fig. 97.

Fig. 26

LINGUISTIC ATLAS OF ENGLAND

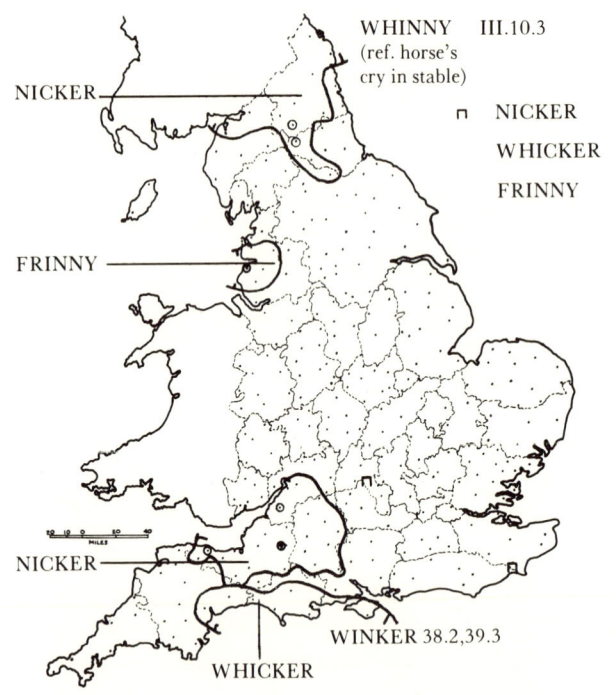

WHINNY III.10.3
(ref. horse's cry in stable)

NICKER

⊓ NICKER
WHICKER
FRINNY

FRINNY

NICKER

WINKER 38.2, 39.3
WHICKER

Note. NICKER is in gen. use fr. Chesapeake Bay to southern Ohio & Kentucky, & sometimes in New England; WHICKER rec. southeastern New England, Maine, Lower Susquehanna, southern 2/3 of Delmarvia, Virginia, Tidewater & the Carolinas. W.G.E.U.S., p. 64 & Fig. 97.

Fig. 27

LINGUISTIC ATLAS OF ENGLAND

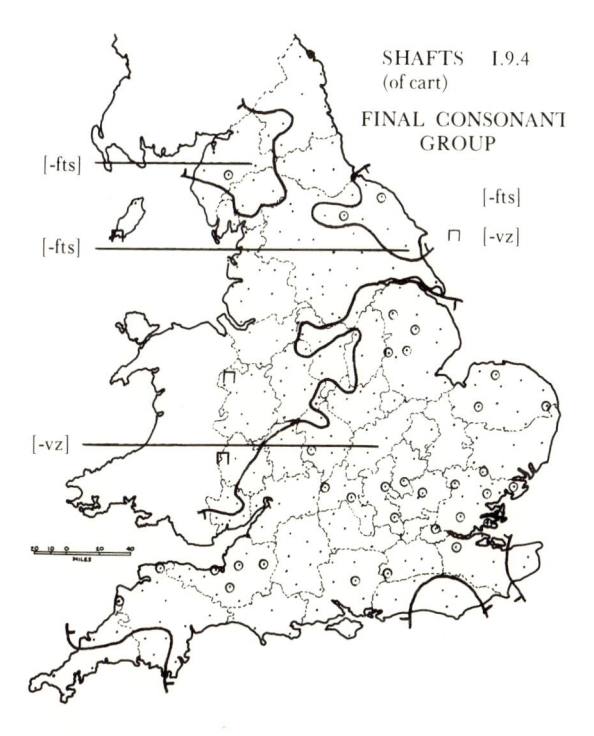

SHAFTS I.9.4
(of cart)
FINAL CONSONANT GROUP

[-fts]

[-fts]

[-fts]

[-vz]

[-vz]

Note. See W.G.E.U.S., p. 17.

Fig. 28

LINGUISTIC ATLAS OF ENGLAND

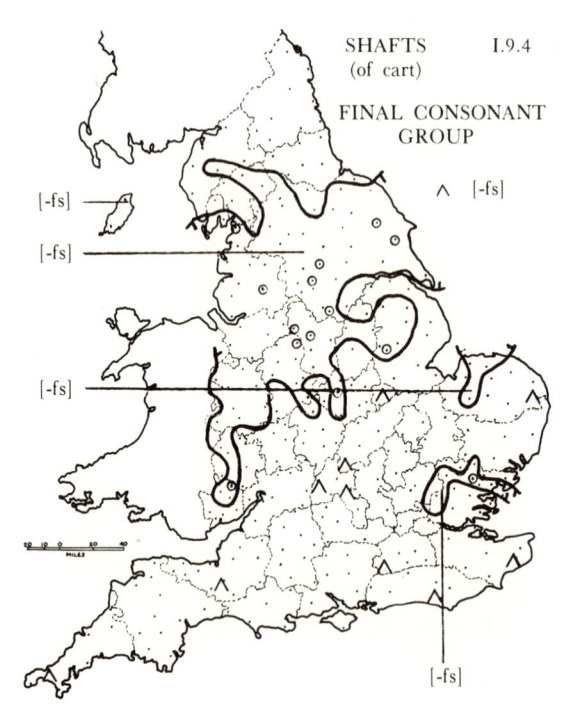

SHAFTS I.9.4
(of cart)

FINAL CONSONANT GROUP

[-fs]

Note. See W.G.E.U.S., p. 17.

Fig. 29

LINGUISTIC ATLAS OF ENGLAND

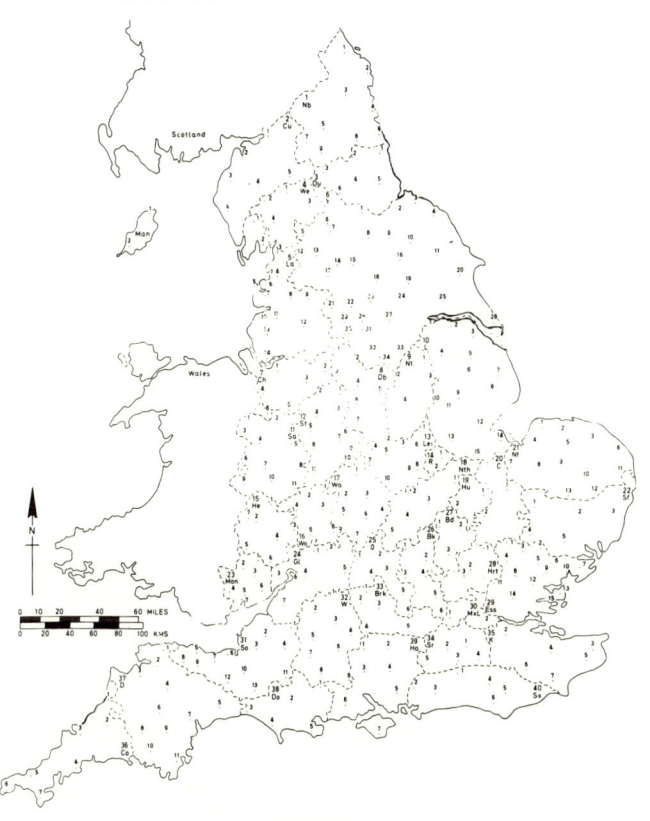

Fig. 30

Part II

Editorial Approaches to Fieldwork Data

WHY NOT A COMPUTER AS EDITOR?

Gordon R. Wood

Southern Illinois University, Edwardsville

¶ All investigators of natural language know that when the last record has been gathered the monumental task of sorting and interpreting the evidence lies ahead. If the evidence is in the form of tape recordings, field notes, or a combination of both, the thought that the details must somehow manually be put into piles according to place of interview, persons chosen, content of response and so on is bound to discourage the hardiest scholars. Judging from the published analyses of the files of the Linguistic Atlas of the United States and Canada, one must limit himself to a single kind of study at a time: pronunciation of selected words in New England, the location of some local words in the Atlantic states, the variables among verbs, or the ranges of individual pronunciation of stressed vowels and diphthongs. Each of these is obviously related to each of the others, but each was published in its own volume. And a full scale, detailed study of interrelationships of each kind of evidence has yet to be made.

A tireless clerical helper is needed to bring together the riches of evidence in the Linguistic Atlas collection or in any other body of linguistic data. As my title suggests, the digital computer is that helper. Of course there are some readers who will feel that a computer can not be trusted to keep track of one's charge account and so, obviously, can not be used to sort and tabulate important evidence about a language. They have a point. But I offer counter evidence in this essay—evidence which shows how some researchers have used computers and which suggests that computers open the way to new kinds of dialectology.[1]

---

[1] Except as noted below, text examples are from this author's computer processing of two kinds of regional evidence of American English: that obtained by printed questionnaire and that by tape recorded response to a pictorial interview. Full

To begin with, a computer can keep track of all details about the source and the particulars of each utterance. The first step that the researcher takes is to convert his field records into a form that the computer can read. Since most of us are familiar with the punch card, let us use that as our starting point. And let us assume that we are in the process of converting one of thirty tape recorded interviews into a conventionally spelled transcription. These will be punched (with their typed equivalent for human readers) letter for letter, along with identification of the person, his residence, and other identifying details in card after card; the data cards themselves will be numbered serially so that nothing can be misplaced.

Imagine this as a sentence from one informant: "They're just like—well—it was—was sort of like it was when God had Moses ataking the children of Israel out of Egypt." The person saying that would have been given a code that would keep his record apart from that of every other person whose record would be transcribed. In this instance the code is B (for a group of fifteen counties), 201 (for the county and the person), and X (for his age and education). The setting would be identified: 0680, the illustrative identification number, comes from a picture shown to each informant at this stage in the interview. After these are punched in the first eight columns of the first card, the machine will duplicate that coding on all successive cards until the code of the next person is introduced into the collection. Thus each code is duplicated mechanically until a change is introduced.

The text then follows. And here the researcher has a choice of using normal spacing or of putting each word in a column of its own. But he must not use all eighty columns since the last four (or some other arbitrary number) must be reserved for sequence numbering. The second pattern of spacing is illustrated here:

| B201X0680 | WAS | SORT | OF | LIKE | 15 |
| B201X0680 | WAS | WHEN | GOD | HAD | 16 |

---

analysis of the first is in *Vocabulary Change: A Study of Variation in Regional Words in Eight of the Southern States* (Southern Illinois University Press, Carbondale and Edwardsville, 1971). Partial analysis of the taped data is in *Sub-Regional Speech Variations in Vocabulary, Grammar, and Pronunciation* (photo offset. Southern Illinois University, Edwardsville, 1967), now available as Document ED 019 263, ERIC Document Reproduction Service.

```
B201X0680  MOSES     ATAKING  THE  CHILDREN  17
B201X0680  OF        ISRAEL   OUT  OF        18
```

This format leaves a lot of unused space between words, space that in computer storage will be filled with blanks. But it does have the advantage of letting the researcher punch special codes after specific words if he wishes to do so at a later time.

Those punched cards, read into the machine one at a time, will let the computer store that information in such a way that each instance of *was, of, ataking,* and the like can be counted and identified as belonging to informant B201X. That count can be then put into ascending numerical order or into alphabetical order or both. And, as the total group of responses is enlarged, the responses of those whose age and education is coded A or M or Q can be compared with each other and with that coded X above.

Out of necessity, in the past dialectology has selected words like *ataking* and has ignored those like *was,* which presumably had a general occurrence in all dialects. If by chance a word like *to* was selected, the choice was governed by the presence of obvious contrasts as in *sick to—, sick at—,* or *sick on his stomach.*

Computers extend the range of possible comparison and, as counting machines, provide indices to regional relationships that could not be found readily by manual tabulation. Consider, for instance, the concording program which can sort and alphabetize every word in a text. One such is called KWIC Sort, an acronym for "key word in context." This program causes the alphabetized text to be printed so that the key word is centered in a segment of context; all instances of the word are counted and become the base of computations. In the *h* segment, for example, the single instance of the word *hive* would appear thus as text:

GETTING HONEY OUT OF A HIVE HITCHED, ATTACHED TO B292G1903

The number of sources and the number of occurrences appear immediately below the text proper. In alphabetical sequence seventeen instances of *his* and one of *hitched* were listed before it and twenty-four occurrences of *hog* after it. Two of the latter will serve to show the format of the text with identification codes removed:

HUNDRED AND NINETY TWO A HOG EATING APPLES LOOKS LIKE
TWO WE HAVE AN OLD HOG UNDER AN APPLE TREE AND

With examples, numbers, and percentages of occurrence before us we are in a better position to describe the total dialect than we are when we depend solely on selected regional words. With *his, hitched, hive,* and *hog* as counted instances we can begin to formulate sounder hypotheses about dialect features than we have been able to do up to this point. But what if researchers wish to follow the investigative techniques associated with the Linguistic Atlas of the United States and Canada? The answer is that computers provide excellent clerical help in handling the data.

One range of possibilities can be shown by considering evidence obtained by the use of printed questionnaires. For those who do not know this tool, the questionnaire consists of directions, a check list, and a biographical page. A number entry, 34 for instance, could be identified in the questionnaire as "an iron cooking utensil" and the synonyms named there could be *creeper, fryer, frying pan, skillet,* and *spider.* This entry, always bearing the same identifying number and containing the same words in the same order, could be coded as 34.1, 34.2, 34.3, and so on. With these codes already stored, the word *creeper* would automatically be changed to 34.1 each time the machine read a card in which the informant's chosen answer *creeper* had been punched. All of which may seem unduly cumbersome. Not at all, so far as machine functions are concerned. It is easier for the machine to match the same number sequence than it is to match letter sequences. In this instance the code 34 keeps all the synonyms together while the numeral 1 immediately serves to distinguish *creeper* from its fellows and 2 and 3 serve to distinguish *fryer* from *frying pan,* a pair that matches for the first three letters.

The coded words along with their biographical tags can then be called from storage in different arrangements. Assume that the researcher wishes to test hypotheses about the obsolescence of sets of words, he can instruct the computer to print a count according to selected age groups. In effect his question is this: *Do old people choose one word more often than its synonyms?* Since obsolescence is under study in this example, the same question would be repeated for sorted age groups. The researcher could order the computer to print the tabulations as summarized for a large region, such as a state, or as itemized for a county by county comparison. Extracts from three computer printouts are combined here to illustrate the kind of detail that could appear for *creeper* (item 34.1) and *fryer* (34.2).

	AGE 70, 80, 90		AGE 40, 50, 60		AGE 20−, 30, 40	
	Item 34.1	34.2	Item 34.1	34.2	Item 34.1	34.2
County						
WHITE	0	1	0	1	0	0
ROAN	1	1	0	0	0	1
RHEA	1	1	0	1	0	1

The reader might suppose that such computer lists would serve the scholarly community best if they were copied directly by photography and published (perhaps in microfiche). But one has only to recall the number of counties even in the smallest states and the thousand or so separate synonyms in a questionnaire to realize that the document would probably be too bulky for general distribution. Qualified scholars might want to examine the original printout sheets. If they have had any experience with computers, however, they would ordinarily prefer to have the computer bring the details together in a more manageable form. That is, the computer records of these details are best handled by mechanical rather than human inspection.

Computer summaries of the detailed evidence, however, are of considerable usefulness. The researcher will have to decide on the format and on how the computer printout will be handled. Some instances can clarify the problems.

Informants were asked to add words to the text of the printed questionnaire if they thought that such words should have been included in the original list of synonyms. An alphabetical list seemed the most convenient format. So the computer was instructed to make such a list and to include an identifying number in parentheses and the state from which the word had come. A segment of that list looked like this:

BREAKING UP	(5)	AL AR LA
BREAKING OFF	(5)	AR FL GA TE
BREAST BONE	(69)	FL GA TE
BRICK BAT	(64)	TE
BULL FROG	(9112)	MI
BULLFROG STRANGLER	(6)	FL OK

The two-letter abbreviations are the codes for Alabama, Arkansas, Florida, Georgia, Louisiana, Mississippi, Oklahoma, and Tennessee. It should be obvious by now that the list could have been arranged by interview number or by states listed separately, if the researcher had so wished.

A different consolidation is that of numerical frequency beginning with zero and going to the largest number of reported instances of the words under investigation. Of course, zero counts are possibly *only* when the researcher uses a printed questionnaire since he can scarcely conduct a spoken interview which includes the question "You don't use this word ever do you?" For printed interviews, however, a zero response equals a positive statement that the entire population sample has rejected this specific word. An instance from an early count will serve; a later, corrected count was published, but this is accurate for purposes of illustration. Representative words rejected by 1,000 or more informants were:

> EACEWORM
> CREEPER
> HAY DOODLES

The first listed for one, two, and three choices respectively were:

> 1 DOMINIE
> 2 ANGLEDOG
> 3 WARTY TOAD

Frying pan appeared in the words chosen by three hundred to four hundred persons.

> 353 EARTHWORM

356 SHAVS
357 COURT
359 FRYING PAN
363 DOWNPOUR

These four words end the list and indicated the grand total of informants:

1060 RAIL FENCE
1065 PALLET
1068 LIGHTNING BUG
1094 HAYSTACK

Gross counts of this sort raise all sorts of interesting questions about the usage labels that dictionary makers assign to words—labels like *dialectal, sub-standard, Southern*. Though he will not get any usage labels, the researcher with a computer can ask questions about the local relationships of these words to each other and can get a reply in percentages, a reply which may be more informative to him and to other researchers than are the numbers or labels themselves. With reference to the controlled universe of questionnaire entries, one can ask how the state total of choices of one word relates to a regional total. Or he can ask how the number of choices within the state relates to the greatest possible number of choices there. Or, again, if the state total is set at one hundred percent, how do choices in the northern or eastern half compare with those in the southern or western half? Or, finally, if one has the state totals for all choices among a set of synonyms, how does one synonym relate in terms of the preferences to the choices of the other synonyms?

The computer can then be instructed to carry out the calculations which are required and to print the results so that readers will know the place of each word in the questionnaire and the state or local percentages under each of the separate kinds of calculation. An excerpt ready for photocopying will illustrate this kind of computer compilation. The printout segment illustrated here contains the item number from the questionnaire, the work sheet number for those who use worksheets for the Linguistic Atlas

```
ITEM (34)
WORK SHEET (17)
                        TENNESSEE        GEORGIA           ALABAMA
                         A      B         A       B         A      B
CREEPER                                (NO RESPONSE)
                                       (NO RESPONSE)
                                       (NO RESPONSE)

FRYER              W    **     **    N   30      .3       **     **
                   E    **     **    S   40      .4       10     .1
                   ST   **     **        70       1       10     .1

FRYING PAN         W    11      3    N   18       5        9      3
                   E    19      6    S   19       6        5      2
                   ST   30      9        37      11       14      4

FRY PAN            W    29     .2    N   14      .1       **     **
                   E    14     .1    S   14      .1       **     **
                   ST   43     .3        29      .2       **     **

SKILLET            W    20      8    N   13       5        7      3
                   E    38     15    S    6       2        2      1
                   ST   57     22        18       7        9      4

SPIDER             W     2     .1    N    7      .3        2     .1
                   E     5     .2    S   44       2       **     **
                   ST    7     .3        51       2        2     .1
```

project, and the full list of synonyms given in the questionnaire; descending order corresponds to left to right order of the text. To the right of the word list are letters ST (for state total), E, W, N, S for the major state divisions east and west or north and south. Percentages of responses are listed under state headings; here only three of eight states are shown. Immediately underneath the state name are columns identified by letters of the alphabet. Column A gives the state total as a percent of a larger regional total; Column B gives the individual word total as a percent of the maximum number of possible choices in that state if everyone had chosen that word. The entry (NO RESPONSE) is self explanatory; it is used when no informant in any of the eight states has chosen it. The entry ** opposite FRYER means the same thing but is used when the word is reported somewhere else in the whole region under investigation. Double zeros could have been used but it was believed that 00 could be misread more easily than **.

The alphabetic and numerical lists and the complex tabulations which appear above form texts ready to go directly from the computer to the printer for photocopying and publication. The computations will not require proofreading when the galleys come back. At the same time one should take care that the text to be photographed does not contain human errors such as the spelling of *Florida* as *Flordia*, an error that led to my rerunning a vast number of computations.

Direct interviews can be stored in part like the responses to a printed questionnaire. But they demand some special handling. In the first place even though the transcribed words are spelled conventionally, their order of occurrence is unpredictable. That is, the answer *unless* might be given by itself or it might follow or precede *withouten, thouten,* or *lessen*.[2] One way to handle that kind of variation is to give to each word a code so that *unless, without, lessen,* and *thouten* would be punched and coded as UWOLTN. This choice puts a burden on the researcher who must keep track of the basic words and their variant codes as he goes along. It is more systematic to punch the words and have the computer arrange them alphabetically in a restricted dictionary. The size of the dictionary is kept small since each new topic for which responses occur can be kept distinct from the dictionaries arising from other sections of the interview. Then the computer can be instructed to keep only the first two letters of the word and two numerals, a greater convenience for its operations. *Lessen* would then be mechanically converted to LE00 every time it was reported, while *unless* would be UN00. These machine-coded words with their identification numbers would be handled in any way that the researcher wanted them to be. After specified counting and other calculations had been completed, then the coded words would be passed back through the dictionary and converted to their original full form. The printed lists of words, places, and totals resemble those already illustrated above except for the fact that no record could be developed of zero responses.

---

[2] Details from Roger W. Shuy, "An Automatic Retrieval Program for the Linguistic Atlas of the United States and Canada," in *Computation in Linguistics*, eds. Paul L. Garvin and Bernard Spolsky (Bloomington: Indiana University Press, 1966), pp. 60–75. This collection of essays is valuable for those who wish to discuss with programmers the problems of machine handling of data from natural languages.

Phonological evidence of whatever sort presents difficulties in coding and in computer processing. The design of computers causes any tiny difference in a symbol to assume critical importance. To the human being the pairs *her* and *hers*, *hope* and *hoped*, and *unless* and *'less* have most details in common. So far as computer matching goes, each is a distinct word and as such does not match its companion any more than it matches any of the other words named. Of course, there are ways to get around this difficulty but it must be recognized before the researcher decides on his procedure in handling phonetic evidence.

Let us assume that the key punch and machine require him to use only the familiar upper case alphabet and a half dozen additional signs such as the numerals. Literal computer A, then, will probably serve two functions: it will stand for /a/ of *hot* and /æ/ of *hat*. The first sound will be distinguished by the coded addition of zero and the second by the numeral one. As punched the words would be HA0T and HA1T and would be kept separate by the contrast in the machine record for 0 and 1. But let us assume further that for other speakers the two words are almost diphthongs. If the glide concluding the diphthong is coded 9, then HA09T and HA19T would still be kept apart from each other as well as from the forms coded without the glide. At this point the researcher will have to instruct the computer to ignore the 9 when it comes to classifying the variants of *hot* under one phonic head and those of *hat* under another. Restated, for the computer HA0T does not match HA09T and some instruction must be given if the match is to succeed.

Restrictions of various sorts are imposed by the computer at hand, the programs or sets of instructions for that computer, and the funds that one can obtain. Assuming no restrictions, the researcher who has made finely graded phonetic transcriptions must still ask himself whether it is worth the time and effort to put them into a code that the machine can read. Is it best to have the machine simplify and generalize the coded transcription before matching words for their phonic or phonemic shapes? If so, what use is to be made of the original fine details which are stored on the punch cards and in computer memory? Considering this special oddity of computer matching, would it not be better to code in a phonic format in the first place? These and other questions will have to be solved locally before the user can feel that computer analysis of the transcribed spoken record is comparable with the analysis of conventionally spelled words themselves.

Regardless of the detail, the researcher will at some time wonder whether his machine counts cannot be converted into some form other than that of word lists and percentage tables. Obviously if the evidence can be counted, it can also be shown as graphs and maps. The sole requirement is that the researcher have access to a device which will plot the counted evidence. With what is called a digital plotter, W. N. Francis and his colleagues prepared some impressive maps of the occurrence of fricatives in the Southern British dialect.[3] Choosing data from the Orton survey, they instructed the computer to draw maps of various patterns of occurrence. Map 9, reproduced here with permission of the authors, shows the variations in the word *thistle*. An eastern cluster is mainly /θ/, a western one /d/, and between are / ð , v, s/.

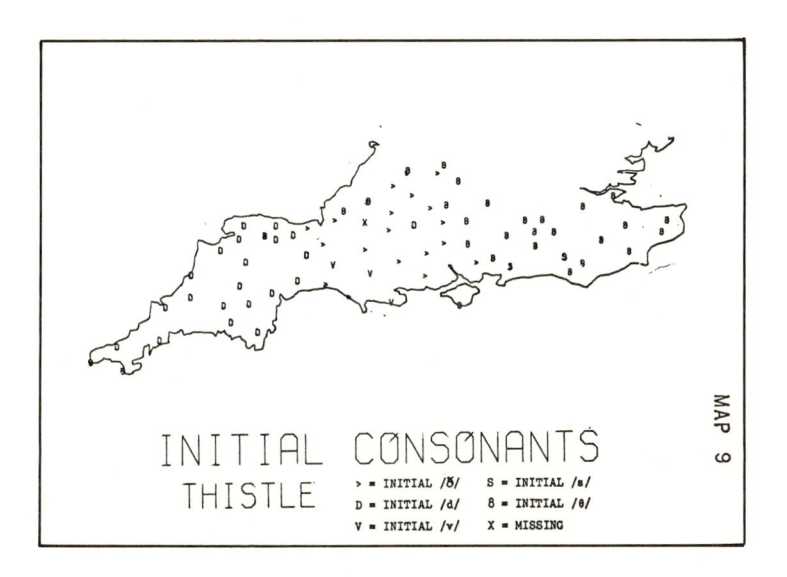

INITIAL CONSONANTS
THISTLE
> = INITIAL /ð/   S = INITIAL /s/
D = INITIAL /d/   θ = INITIAL /θ/
V = INITIAL /v/   X = MISSING

MAP 9

---

[3] From W. N. Francis, J. Svartvik, G. M. Rubin, *Computer Produced Representation of Dialectal Variation: Initial Fricatives in Southern British English*, Preprint No. 52, International Conference on Computational Linguistics, Stockholm,

If the computer center does not have a plotter or if its use is too expensive, the researcher can employ another technique. It is to instruct the machine to print and overprint selectively letters and other symbols. The resultant map made from single and overprinted symbols might look like this with 0, X, and + representing different linguistic features:

```
0000000000000000XXXXXXXXXXX+++++++++++
000000000000000XOXOXXXXXXXXX+++++++++++
00000000XOXOXOXOXOXOXXXXXXXXXXX+++++XXXXXX+
000000XOXOXOXXXXXX++++XXXXXX+++++++++XXXXX
```

Such a map is so obviously crude that the researcher probably would not want to publish it though he might want to circulate a few copies to his fellow researchers. Still, even in its crude form, the patterns of occurrence are those that result from impartial tallying. Thus the researcher who wishes to move from data to theory does have an objective display of the distribution of data before him.

With the crude map before us we need to think about the computer as apprentice printer. Some emerging details are so densely coded that they would not be reproduced for general use; they are details that are best stored in computer memory for use in later calculations. Other details, simulated in the map above, are sufficiently explicit to aid the researcher and his associates in reaching conclusions. And finally there are details that are sufficiently good to go directly from the computer printout to the publisher's photocopying processes. "Sufficiently good" is a relative term. If readers will turn again to the computations for *creeper* and its synonyms, they will see instances of poorly formed letters and wavy lines of print. This example is by no means the most slovenly page that the

---

1969. Permission to reproduce one of the maps is gratefully acknowledged. One should also consult the computer maps in W. Nelson Francis, "Modal *Daren't* and *Durstn't* in Dialectal English," in *Studies in Honour of Harold Orton on the Occasion of his Seventieth Birthday,* ed. Stanley Ellis (Leeds Studies in English, New Series, II, 1969), pp. 145–63.

For other graphic methods of presenting dialectal data by computer, see Wood, *Dialectology by Computer,* Preprint No. 19, International Conference on Computational Linguistics, Stockholm, 1969.

computer printed. Or, to put it another way, the researcher had to call for four runs of every page in order to get one best page for photocopying. Furthermore when these best pages are brought together, the total result still is a lack of uniformity from one part of the copy to the next.

Readers may have seen publicity about typewriter terminals and special photographic devices which, when joined to a computer, do produce work that resembles letterpress. These devices may not be at hand when the researcher wants to use them, or they may be so costly to use that he will have to settle for the work of the computer as apprentice printer, work of the sort that has been illustrated in this article. But these seem mainly to be esthetic decisions.

As for the decision to use computers in searching linguistic records, listing the materials found there according to some analytical scheme and reporting the evidence, the dialectologist seems to me to have no choice now. His concern is not whether to use the machine but rather how to use it best.

SOME PROBLEMS IN EDITING THE LINGUISTIC ATLAS OF THE UPPER MIDWEST

Harold B. Allen

University of Minnesota

The presentation of data from the continuing research in the regional diversity of American English requires the solution of a number of editorial problems. Some of these did not arise when 35 years ago Hans Kurath pioneered with the editing of the first American regional atlas, that of New England; some that he did face now occur in different circumstances and hence require different answers.

That Kurath's solutions would not necessarily hold for subsequent regional atlases has been recognized for some time. At an informal meeting in New York in 1950 American linguistic geographers agreed that the cartographical opulence of the New England Atlas offered a striking precedent no longer practicable. Its magnificent maps with hand-drawn phonetic symbols, filling three huge folios, set an example hardly to be replicated when production costs of all kinds were already several times higher than at the end of the Depression of the 1930's and when prospects of financial support had become evanescent. The group then met an initial problem of presentation by concurring upon the practical desirability of using, instead of hundreds of hand-fashioned maps, only a few base maps accompanied by tables or lists of informants' responses.

In 1958, hoping that it might soon be possible to begin editing the field records of the Linguistic Atlas of the Upper Midwest, I sent to twelve persons a brief questionnaire requesting comments on a number of specific editing problems that even then could reasonably be anticipated. Perceptive and helpful replies came from nine of them: the late E. Bagby Atwood, Walter Avis, Sumner Ives, the late Majorie Kimmerle, Albert H. Marckwardt, Raven

I. McDavid, Jr., T. M. Pearce, Carroll Reed, and David Reed. These replies, contradictory as they sometimes were, continued the accumulation of fact and opinion that ultimately helped to provide the answers to the editorial problems of the Upper Midwest Atlas. Additional help came from study of the various published European atlases and from visits, supported by a two-year grant from the National Endowment for the Humanities from 1967–1969, to the headquarters of the English Dialect Survey and to the headquarters of the corresponding Scottish Survey. From Harold Orton of the University of Leeds, director of the first, and from J. Y. Mather of the University of Edinburgh, director of the second, came suggestions and information of importance in the step-by-step process of reaching decisions about these problems. Each decision, however, was a function of the editor; and he alone must accept the adverse criticism that ultimately will come from more or less outraged reviewers who would have made other choices—or choose to believe that they would.

Certainly a quite early decision that in effect selected the answers to several later questions resulted from the question, What will be the target audience of the publication? Previous atlas publications, here and abroad, have been for scholars, although the New England Atlas has been followed by two descriptive volumes, *Pronunciation of English in the Atlantic States* and *Word Geography of the Eastern United States,* usable by a wider audience. The Upper Midwest editor has but a limited time remaining before retirement, he has been unable to solicit adequate funds for two separate series of publications, and he has an almost evangelical and perhaps unscholarly desire to encourage the study of American dialects in school and colleges.

For better or for worse, the choice, therefore, was to aim at two targets simultaneously. For scholars the basic data, response by response and informant by informant, will appear so that they can make various categorical analyses in accord with their particular research concerns. For the interested layman, even the selected secondary school student and his teacher, there will be descriptive generalizations with a modicum of non-doctrinal interpretation. But the scholar presumably should find the descriptions of value and the school and college student should be able to make at least superficial use of the data.

What, then, should be the format? Without the need to plan for huge inscribed maps the quarto two-column format already found adequate in Kurath's *Word Geography* seemed to be worth emulating. But a modification developed when arrangements with a publisher occurred. This format, with quite a bit of handset composition and the use of a special phonetic font, would be so expensive as to require subvention of perhaps $8,000. The solution agreed upon with the University of Minnesota Press calls for the submission of final copy such that it can be photographed for photo-offset printing. With practically no cost for composition the Press did not need a subvention. The copy thus provided will be with an unjustified right-hand margin, as in, for example, the *Middle English Dictionary*. To provide such copy the Atlas was able to obtain an IBM Selectric typewriter for which a specially modified Camwill phonetic Selectric element was made.

What material should be included and how should it be treated? These are two different but related questions. The first is complicated by the fact that the Upper Midwest Atlas project is the first to include in its operation the supplementary use of a mail survey. This survey used a checklist of 137 lexical items based upon that used by Alva Davis for his doctoral dissertation. The Upper Midwest files contain the responses of more than 1200 persons from every county but two in the entire five-state area. An early hope to present all this supplementary information, accompanied by the biodata concerning the 1200 respondents, was dashed by the consideration of the space required. Clearly this information could be drawn upon usefully when of value in confirming or denying possibly uncertain results of the field survey, but most of it, being redundant, need not be detailed in the Atlas publication. It may well call for a separate study.

The contract with the University of Minnesota Press calls for the organization of the material into four volumes, although possibly the projected third and fourth volumes may be combined into one. The first volume will be general and introductory, corresponding in many ways to *The Handbook of the Linguistic Geography of New England*. It will include the history and background of the project itself and its relationship to other dialect research in the United States. There will be a description of the field procedures, the questionnaire used, an analysis of the fieldworkers, the history of the population settlement, a bibliography, a description of the communities investigated and of the informants interviewed, and the checklist used in the mail survey. Base maps will indicate the location of the informants and of the mail respondents; other maps will indicate the population growth and the ecological base of the Upper Midwest. The population history is an original study for the Atlas, since none existed for the region. The bibliography, despite the wish of some colleagues that it be comprehensive, will be limited to items relevant to the Upper Midwest, since other resources are now available for other bibliographical listings.

Volume 2 will treat the vocabulary, and it will, of course, have an index. An immediate problem was this. Should lexical items be presented in the original phonetic transcription, as in the New England Atlas and as in Orton's English Survey, or should they be in ordinary orthography? Here the decision was influenced by the value of keeping this content as accessible as possible to readers unaccustomed to phonetic symbols. Except, then, for an occasional transcription to indicate the sound of, say, an animal call, the informants' responses will appear in the usual spelling.

Although the first volume will have offered a general view of the regional patterns, admittedly the thrust of the treatment of vocabulary will be toward the description of the distribution of variants of specific questionnaire items. A number of decisions had to be made before the specific details of the treatment were determined. The result is that a given item will typically contain the following information: (1) cross reference to specific map numbers in the New England Atlas and to specific page and map numbers in the Word Geography; (2) descriptive analysis of the returns, with some reference to the eastern background of the variants and indication of their distribution patterns and relative frequency together with differences among the responses of the three types of informants, if any; (3) all the responses of the field informants, specified by informant number and modified by the use of the familiar symbols for obsolescence, humor, hesitations, use of a secondary informant, and the like; (4) relevant comments made by either the fieldworkers or the informants. Two additional features will sometimes be present. All the 137 items also included in the mail checklist will have a supplementary section describing the returns, sometimes with percentages for the various states and for the Northern and

Midland divisions of Iowa. More than 200 items will be accompanied by small column-width maps.

The use of the maps posed several questions. If the distribution of a variant is quite clearly restricted to a specific area, should that distribution be shown by shading or by an isogloss or by specific informant response symbols? If the distribution is not clearly so delimited, then what? A common Midwest situation reflects the population mixture resulting from some Midland migration into northern Iowa, Minnesota, and North Dakota. Often no isogloss can be drawn at all; rather the picture is simply one of declining Midland frequency and greater Northern frequency as one studies the returns along a vertical axis from the Iowa-Missouri and the Nebraska-Kansas border on the south to the Canadian border on the north. How should this situation be depicted: by shading, by the simple use of response symbols, by percentage figures, by graphs?

The easiest way for me to show you how these questions have been answered is to show some representative maps used to make graphic different kinds of situations. Let's look at eight different kinds.

1. One major form, with scattered minor variants. This common situation is represented by 18.4 *stone boat*, with map symbols (Figure 1).
2. Two major forms, with some minor variants. Examples are 24.4 (Figure 1), *shallow valley*. The first map shows the distribution of the variants, *dry run* and *coulee*. Another instance is provided by 46.7a *angleworm* (Figure 2). Here Kurath's device of using large symbols for the dominating form shows that *angleworm* is the common Northern term; individual symbols mark the incidence of the Midland *fishworm*.
3. Generalized focal items. Sometimes the dialectally significant term is embedded in a compound or a phrase, other members of which may be common to several regions. In such a case the phrases containing one of the contrasting terms can be treated as a homogeneous group. Figure 29.1, for instance, clearly shows that the various *pig* terms and phrases have a Northern orientation; those with *hog* instead of *pig* have Midland orientation (Figure 2).
4. A variant with declining frequency. Sometimes it is desirable to

make graphic the remaining spread of a form which clearly is declining for one reason or another. Illustrations are these maps, one for 16.5a *armload,* a Midland term giving way to Northern *armful,* and one for 17.4 *(wagon) pole,* declining for the simple reason that we no longer hitch a team to a wagon on the farm (Figure 3).
5. Scattered minor variants. To represent a situation in which several lesser variants occur in varied frequency throughout the Upper Midwest, or, contrasting with other variants, in specific subareas, symbols are normally used. Here are a number of illustrative maps indicating the variety to be found in the five-state study.

Figure 4 { 6.7 *chim(b)ley, flue*
7.2 *dog irons*

Figure 5 { 8.1(3b) *lounge, chesterfield*
12.2 *hayrick*

Figure 6 { 12.7(1) *barnlot*
12.7(2) *corral / feed yard* or *lot*

Figure 7 { 12.7(3) Here is the same set as in the preceding map, but now we see the contrast shown by a bar graph. Sometimes each is needed.
13.1 *range*

Figure 8 { 17.5a Northern *fills/thills*
23.6 Midland *comfortable*

Figure 9 { 23.7 So. Midland *pallet* (and *bunk*)
46.2(1) *ground squirrel.* Another case where the jumbo symbol is useful.

6. Dialect merger. Here symbols by themselves do not readily reveal the actual weighting of Northern and Midland forms in the Upper Midwest.

Figure 10 { 4.1 (The sun) *rose/came up*. Use of a piegraph.
32.4 *chick/chickie*. Piegraph.

Figure 11 { 31.7(1) *giddup, giddiap*. The bar graph is not always sufficient.
8.3 *curtains*. Here a combination of bar graph and symbols is useful.

Figure 12 { 8.4a *clothes closet*. Piegraph for this.
29.7 *blat/beller/bawl*. Here a bar graph for three terms.

Figure 13 { 30.3 *setting hen*. Bar graph for four terms (plus symbols).
10.3 *eavestroughs*.

Figure 14 { 9.1 *cleans up*. Bar graph with five terms.
12.5 *hoghouse*. Bar graph with five terms.

Figure 15 { 14.4 *frying pan*. Bar graph with five terms with symbols.
12.3 *haycock*. Bar graph with five terms with symbols.

Figure 16   14.3(1) *slop pail*. Bar graph with six terms.

7. Impinging but not merged subareas.

Figure 16   6.2 (It's) *blowing harder*. Use of isoglosses.

Figure 17   45.8 *snakefeeder.*

8. Earlier distribution of a dying form.

Figure 17   35.7 *doughgod.* Use of the symbol for obsolescence.

As we look ahead to the third and fourth volumes we have not as yet solved the specific problems. The projected third volume will deal with the morphology and the syntax. Certainly the presentation will be influenced by that of the late E. Bagby Atwood in his *Survey of Verb Forms in the Eastern United States.* The fourth volume, that dealing with the phonology, already is causing the greatest difficulty. One problem is the result of the less than adequate transcription of the fieldworkers who did the Iowa records. Another problem is raised by the insistence of the late Uriel Weinreich and Robert Stockwell that dialectologists do a more effective job of interpreting their data. Since Stockwell's article new perspectives have been added by Rudolph Troike and David DeCamp, whose introduction of transformational theory into the interpretation of regional phonetic variations suggests the desirability of explaining the differences in terms of generative phonological rules.

With a wider audience in mind it seems best not to offer only a literal replication of the phonetic transcription in the field records, but rather to attempt a descriptive analysis without intensive reliance upon current phonological theory. For scholars wishing to make further use of the data, the essential evidence will be provided. But generative theory is developing so rapidly that it could easily be quite seriously modified even by the time the fourth volume is published, presumably in 1972. Yet the Upper Midwest Atlas, it is to be hoped, will have a fairly long life as a historical document. In itself it should not rely upon a theoretical analysis that within a few years could be quite outmoded. I hope rather that its contents will be still acceptable in ten, fifteen, or twenty-five years as evidence of the distinctive regional characteristics of Upper Midwest English at the midcentury.

All of the slides utilized in Figures 1–17 have been made available through the courtesy of the University of Minnesota Press, University of Minnesota. They will appear in Volumes 1 and 2 of the *Linguistic Atlas of the Upper Midwest.*

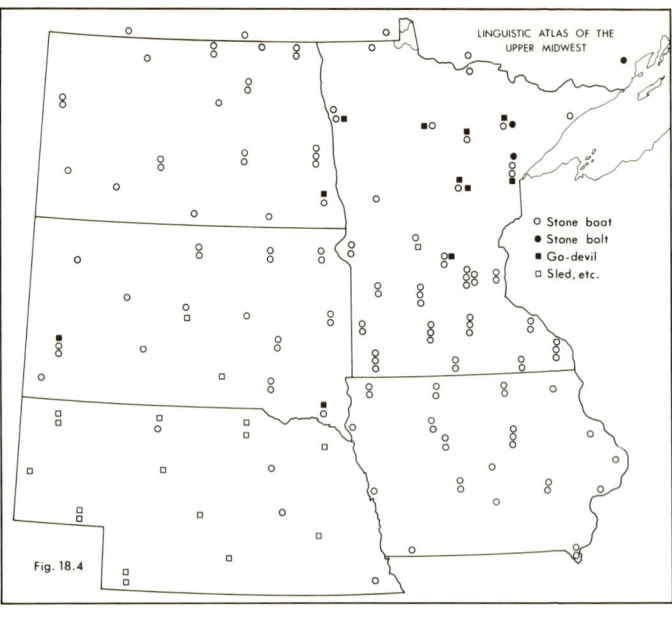

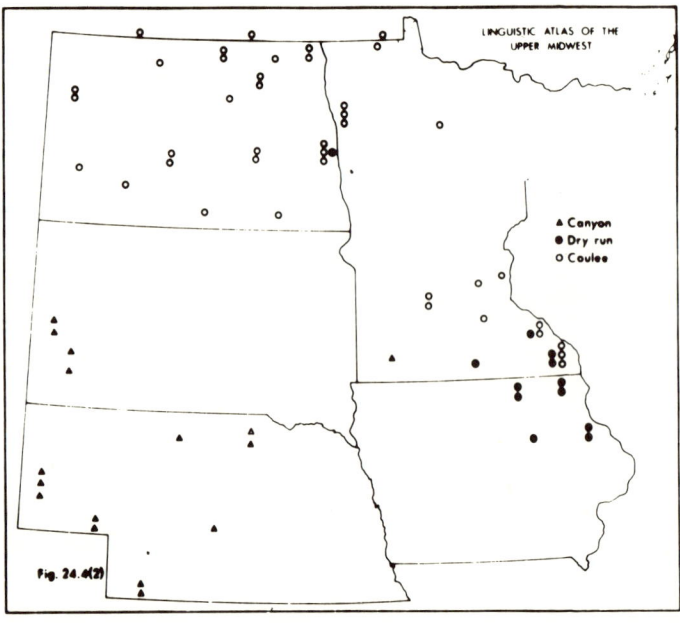

Fig. 1
18.4 stone boat
24.4 (2) canyon

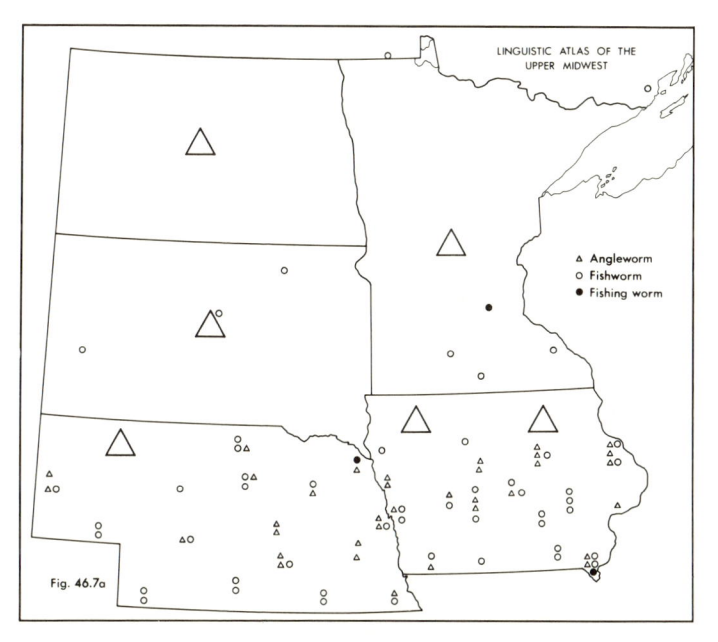

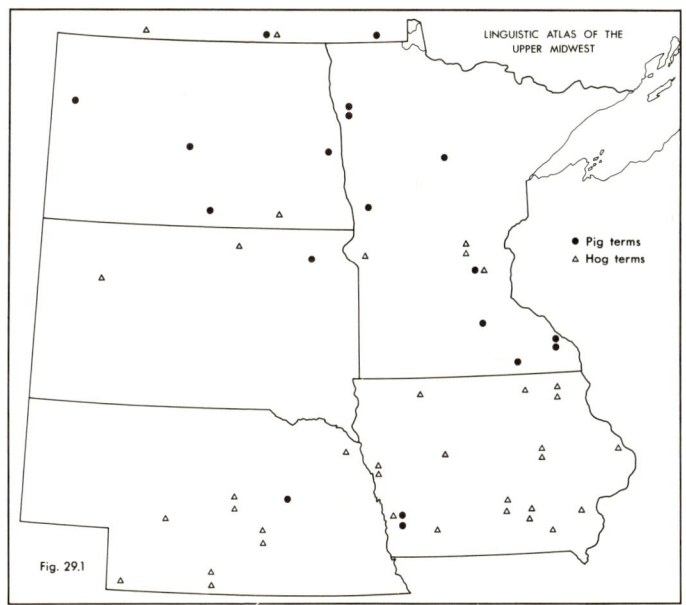

Fig. 2
46.7a Angleworm
29.1 Pig and hog terms

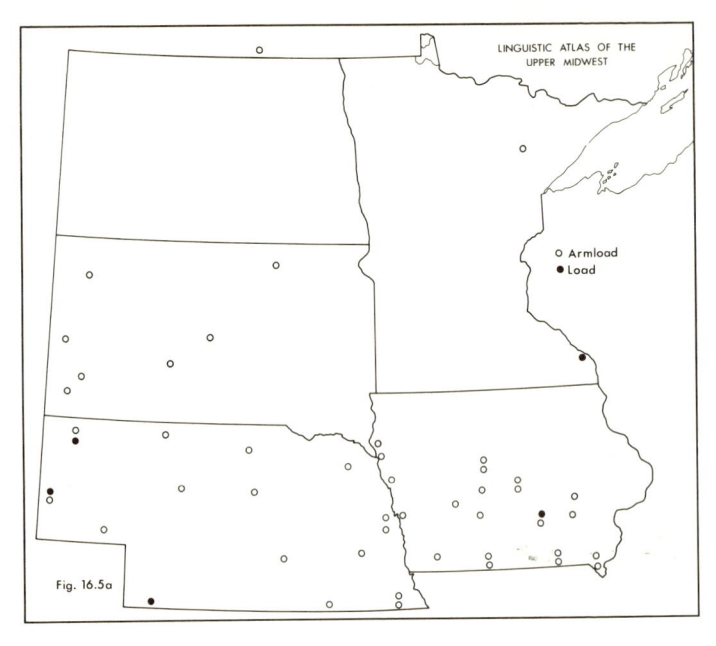

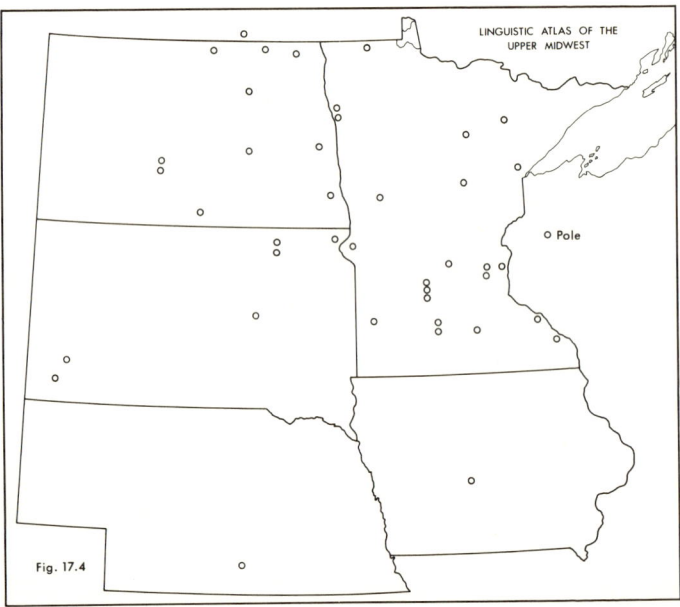

Fig. 3
16.5a armload and load
17.4 (wagon) pole

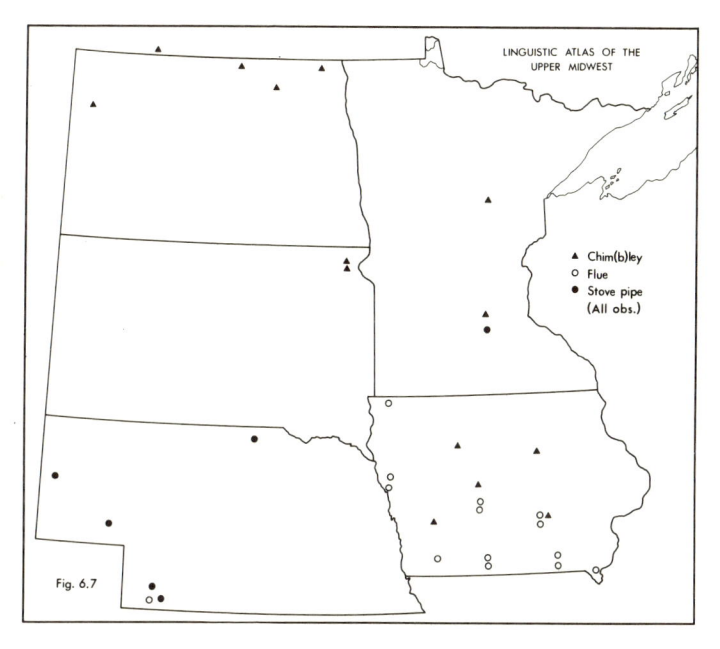

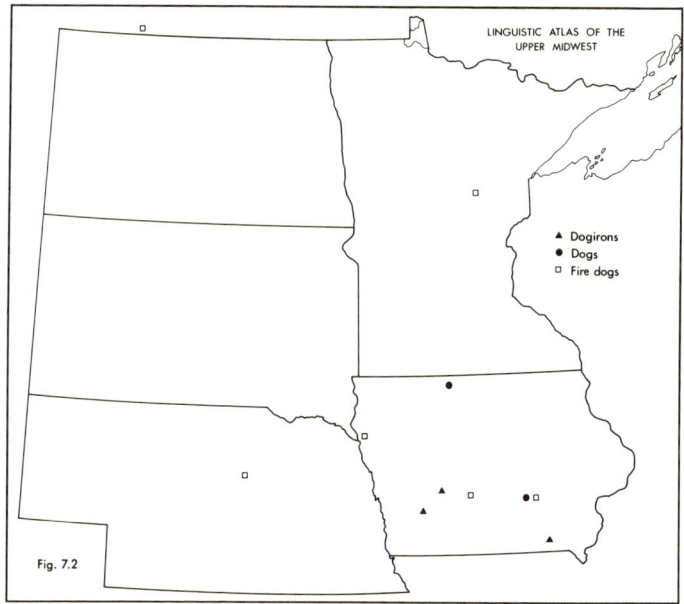

Fig. 4
6.7 chim(b)ley, flue
7.2 dog irons

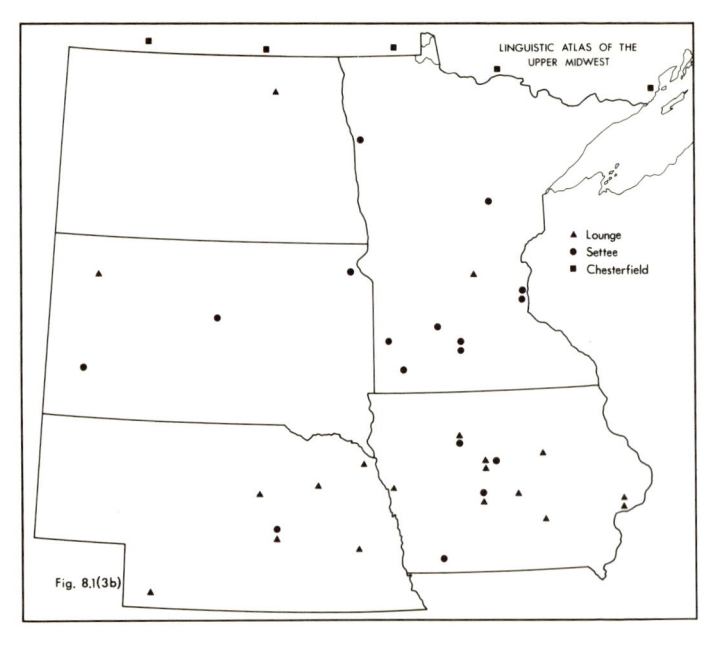

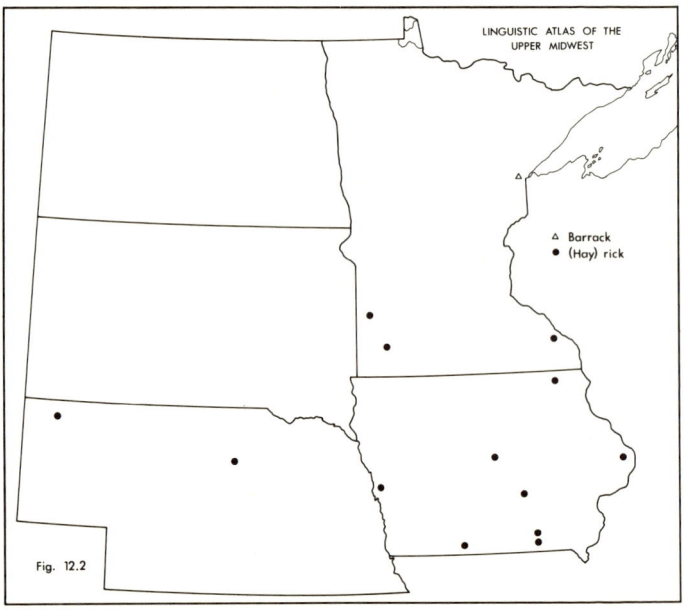

Fig. 5
8.1(3b) lounge, chesterfield
12.2 hayrick

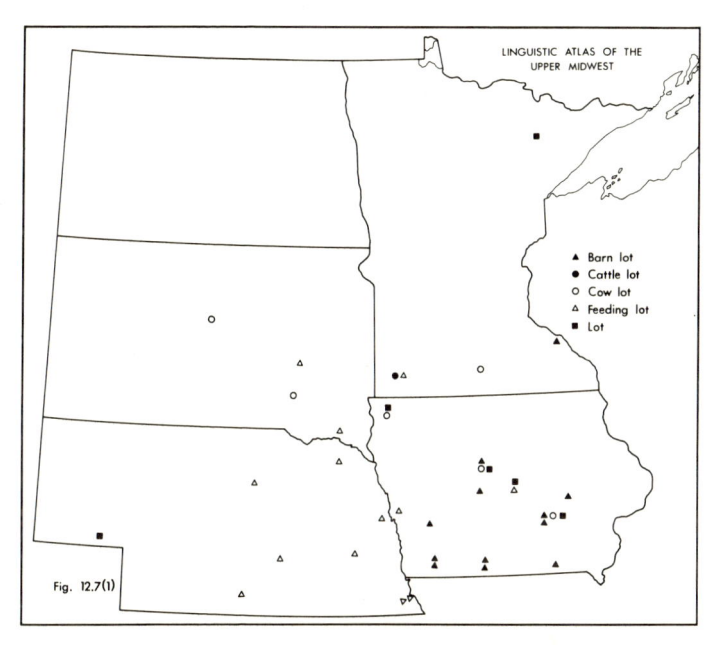

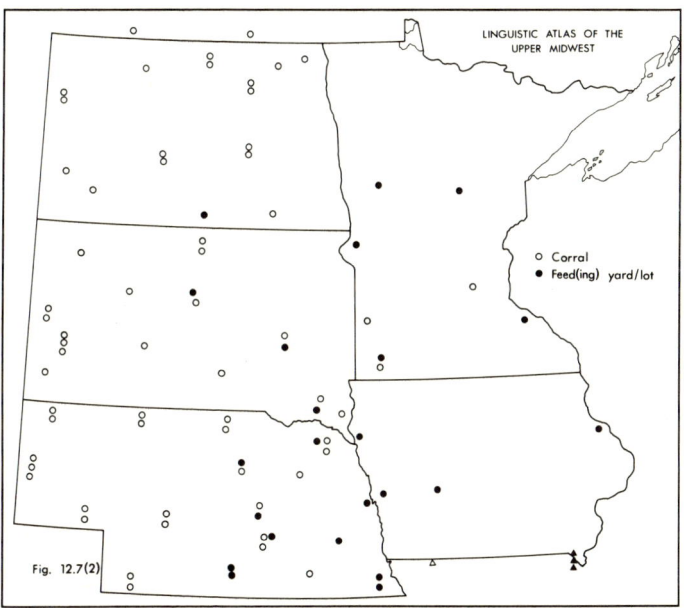

Fig. 6
12.7(1) barnlot
12.7(2) corral/feed yard or lot

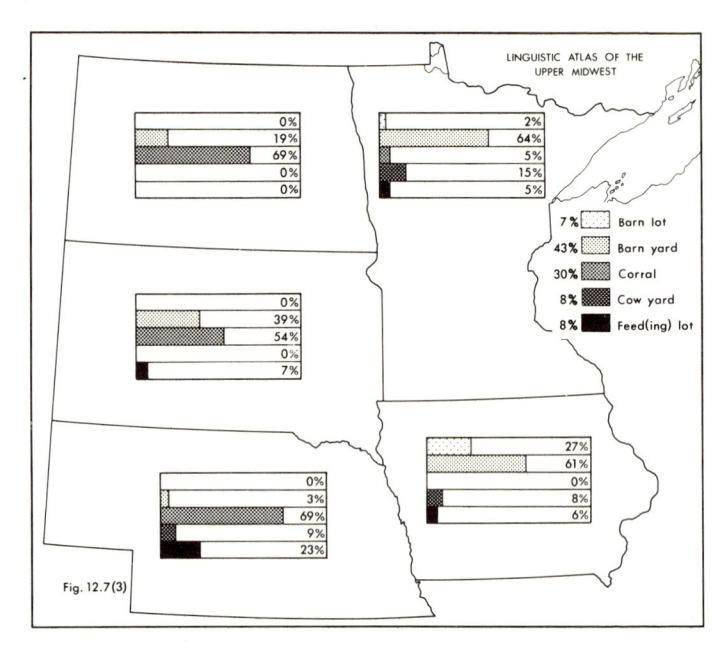

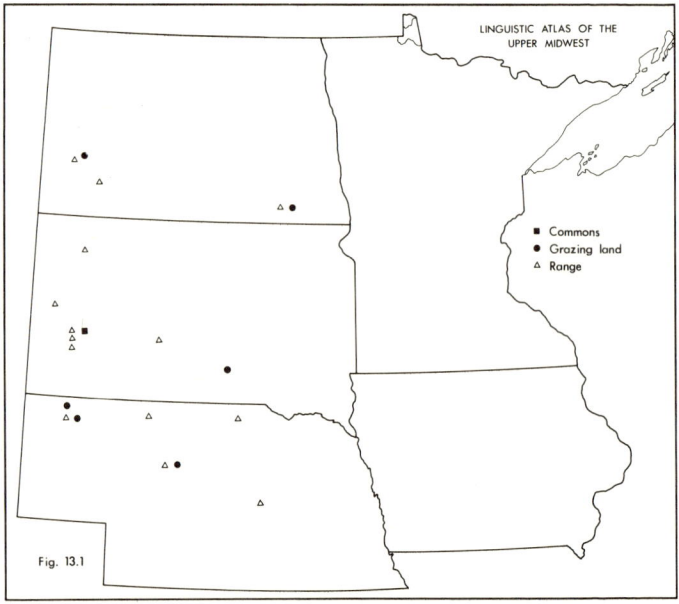

Fig. 7
12.7(3) corral/feed yard or lot on a bar graph
13.1 range

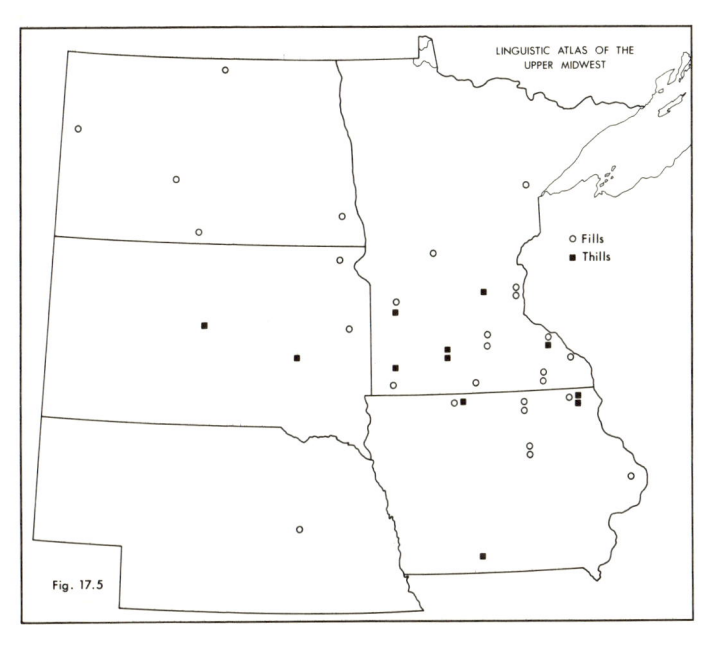

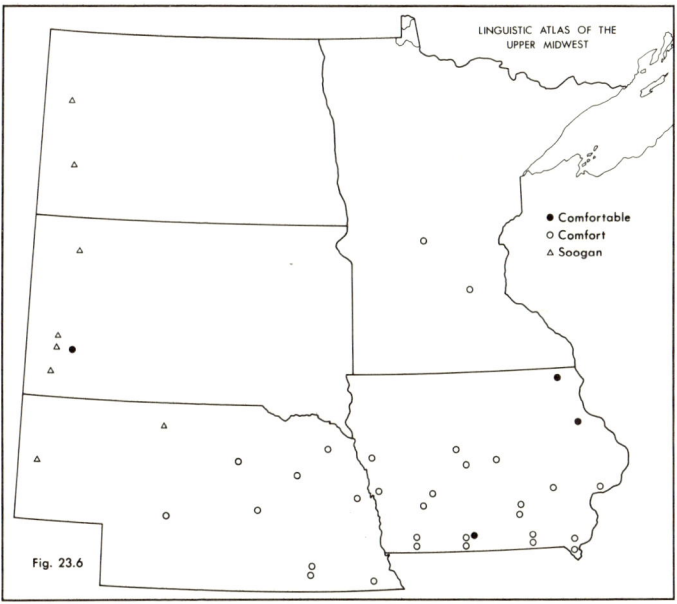

Fig. 8
17.5 Northern fills/thills
23.6 Midland comfortable

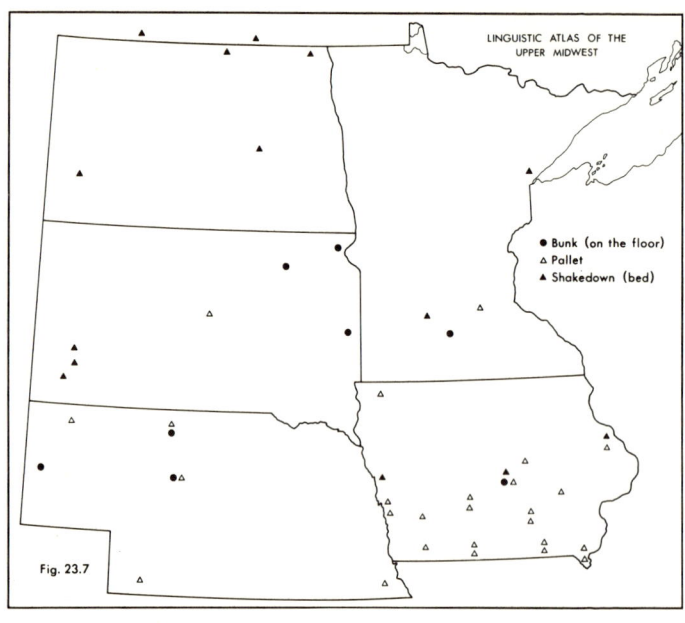

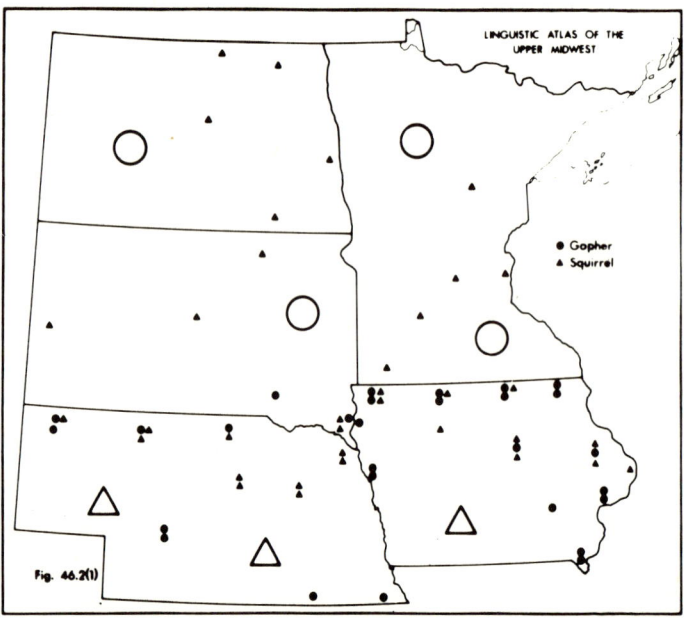

Fig. 9
23.7 South Midland pallet (and bunk)
46.2(1) ground squirrel

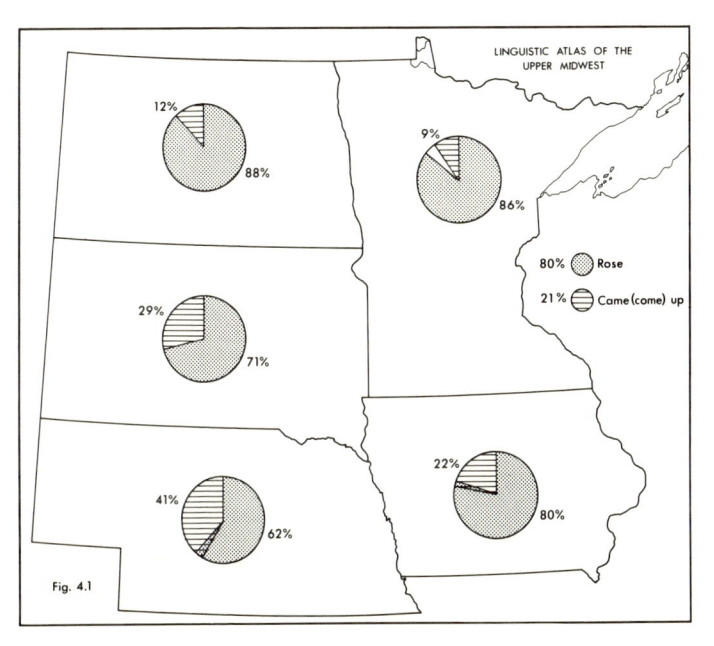

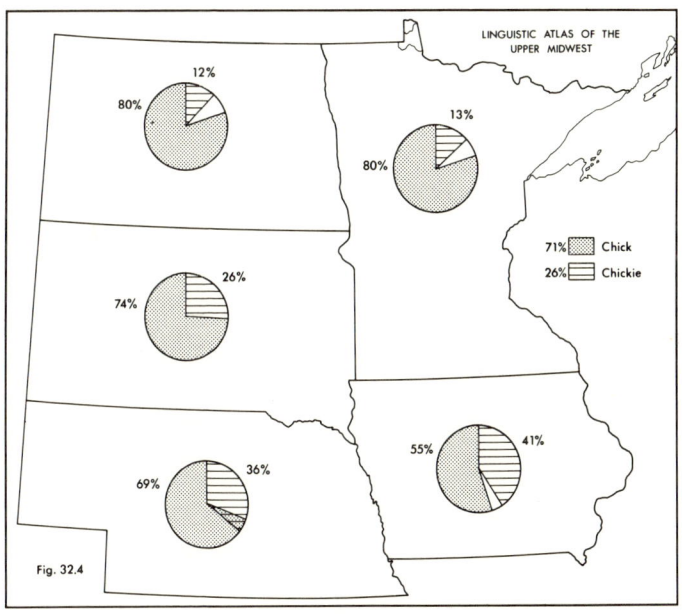

Fig. 10 Piegraphs
4.1 (The sun) rose/came up.
32.4 chick/chickie

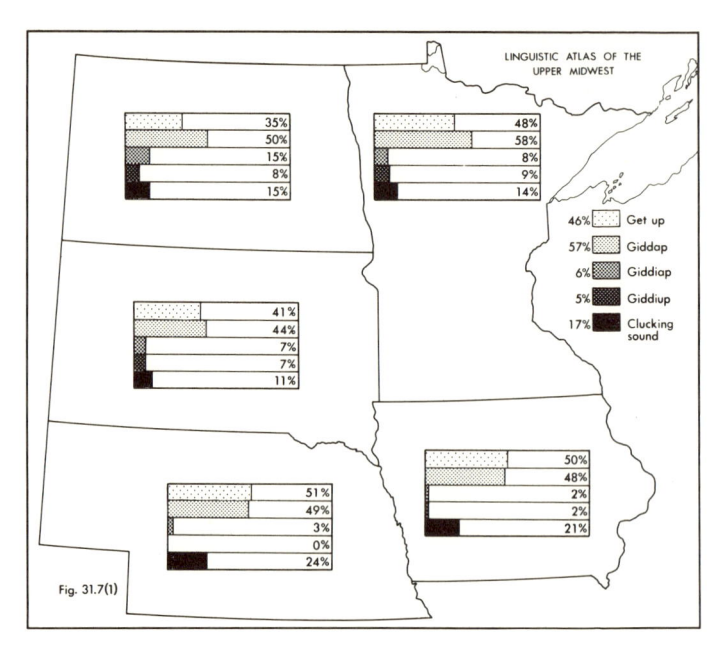

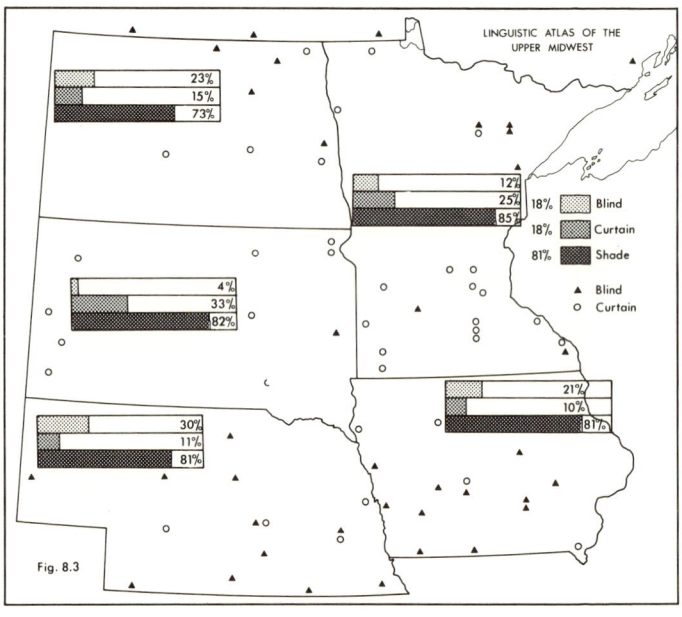

Fig. 11
31.7 (1) giddup, giddiap
8.3 curtains

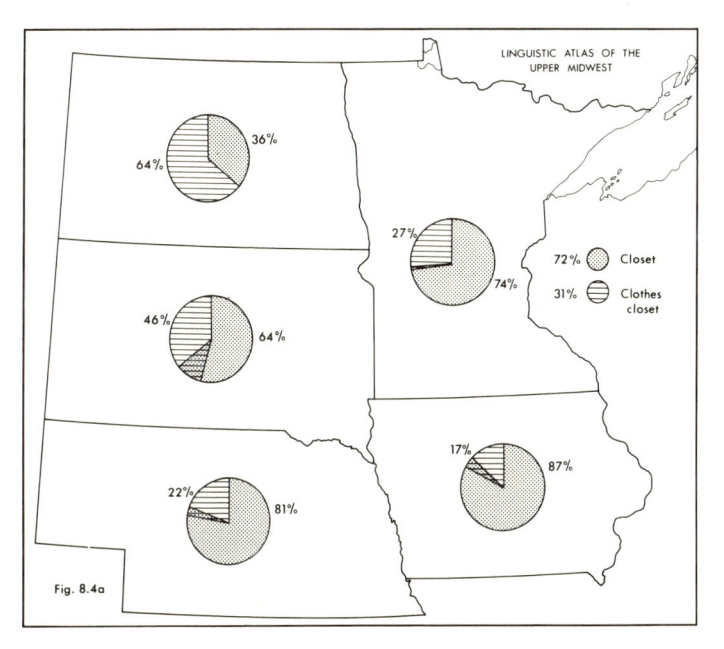

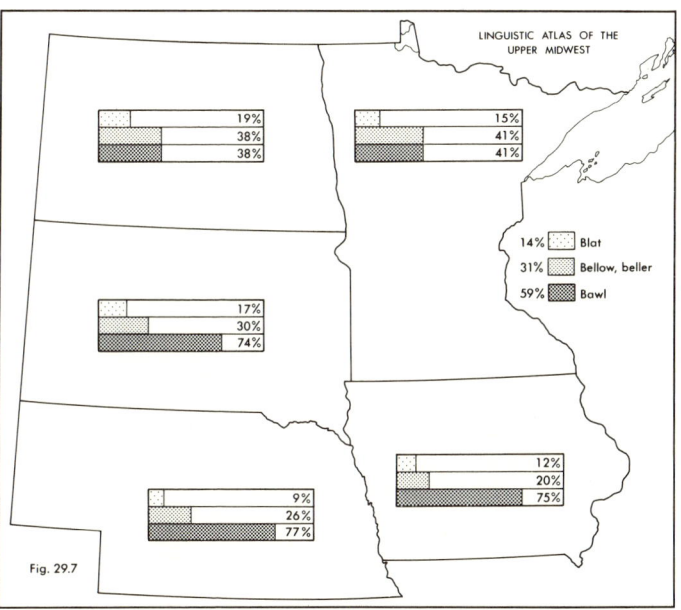

Fig. 12
8.4a clothes closet
29.7 blat/beller/bawl

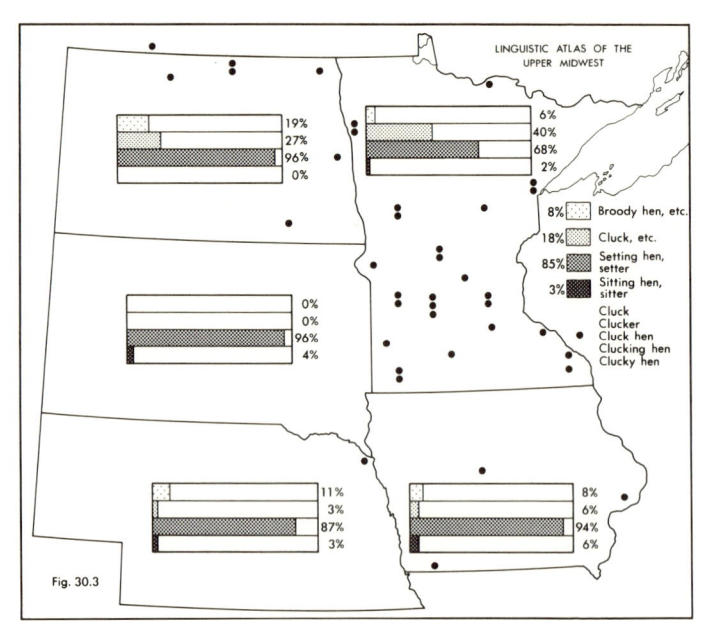

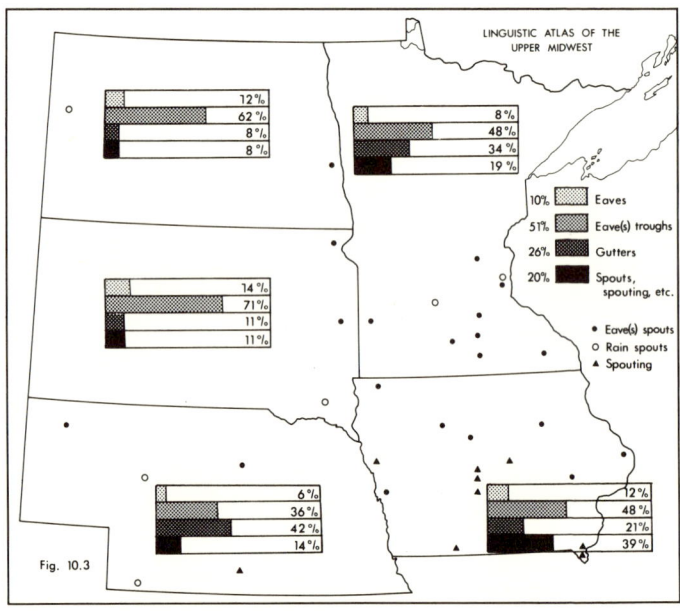

Fig. 13
30.3 setting hen
10.3 eavestroughs

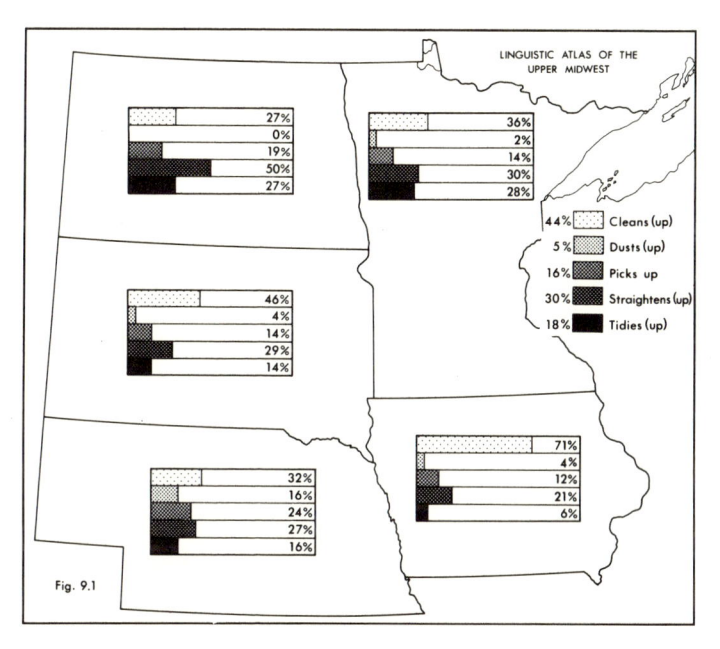

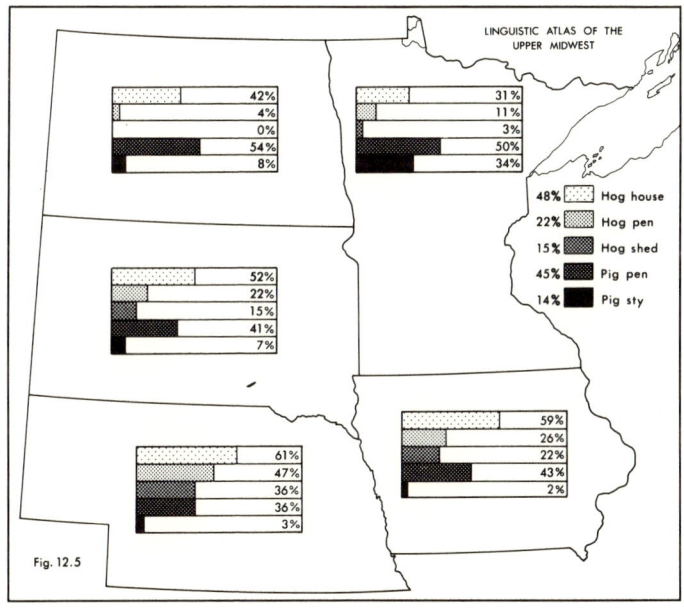

Fig. 14
9.1 cleans up
12.5 hoghouse

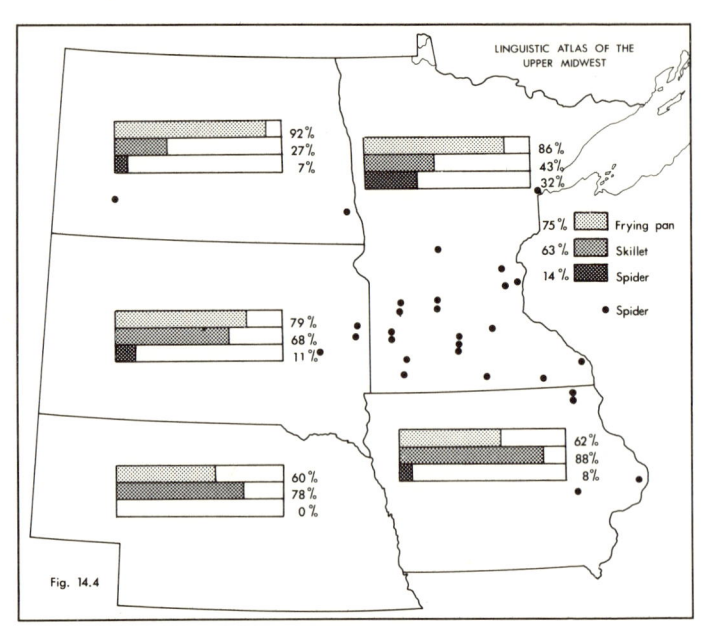

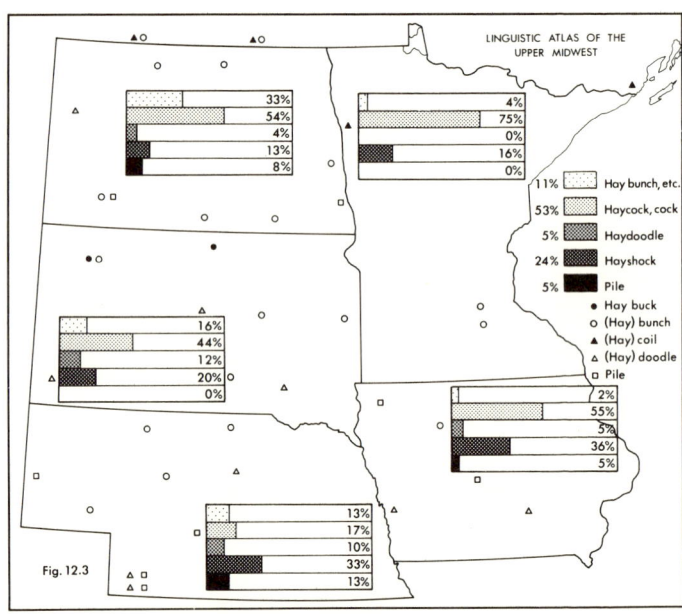

Fig. 15
14.4 frying pan
12.3 haycock

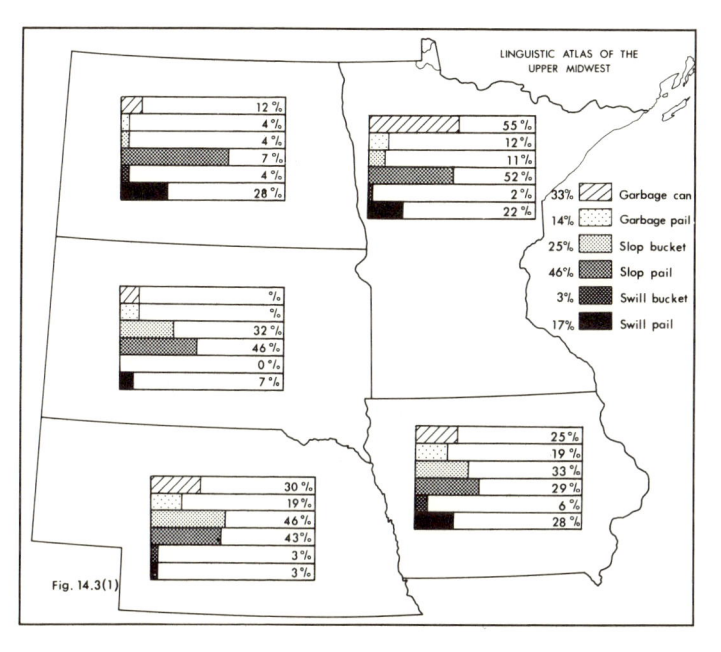

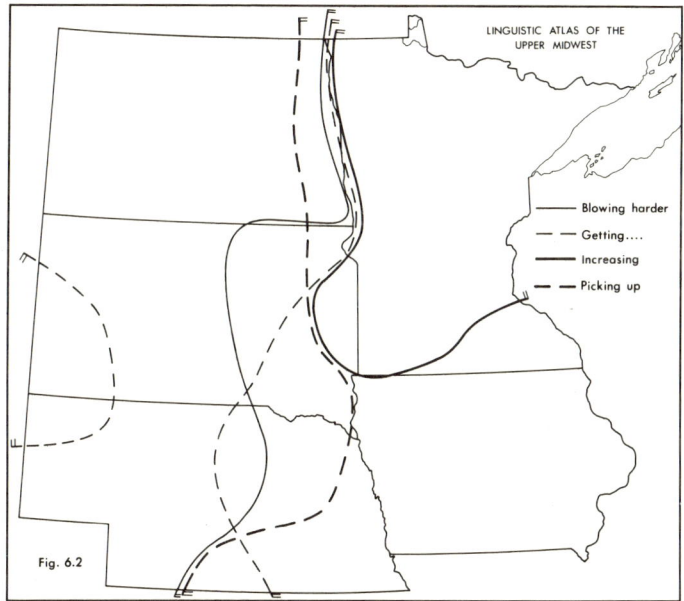

Fig. 16
14.3(1) slop pail
6.2 (It's) blowing harder

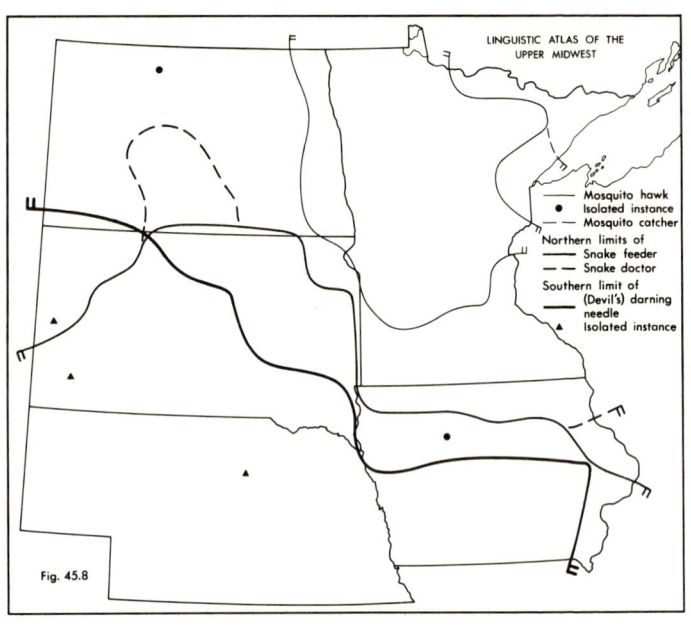

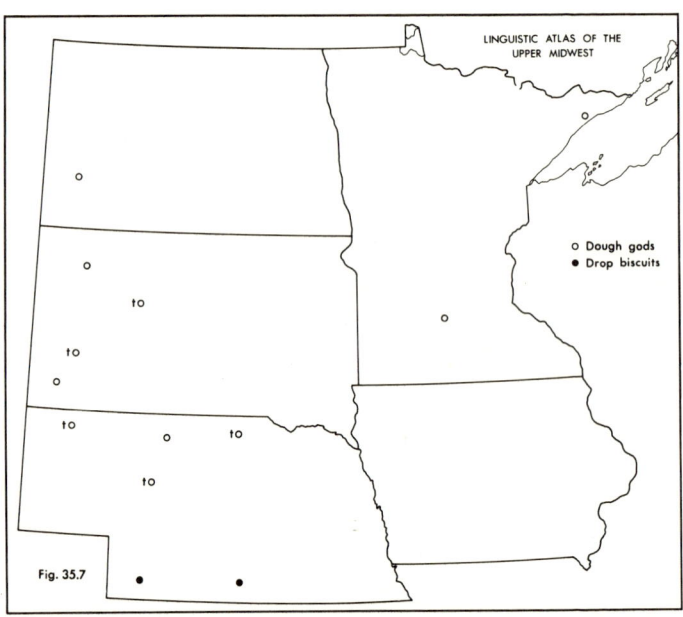

Fig. 17
45.8 snakefeeder
35.7 doughgod

EDITORIAL PROBLEMS OF AN ENGLISH LINGUISTIC ATLAS

Harold Orton

Emeritus Professor, University of Leeds, England
Visiting Professor, University of Tennessee, 1970

¶ To address such an audience as this is for me both a high privilege and most welcome opportunity. The occasion gives me the chance of receiving advice from some of the foremost American dialectologists about my proposals for the *Linguistic Atlas of England* that we shall prepare in the Institute of Dialect and Folk Life Studies in the University of Leeds. Since time now is so short, I shall go straight to my theme.

The material which will form the basis of our Linguistic Atlas comprises over 404,000 items of information. They are the product of just over 1,300 printed questions asked of carefully selected, elderly speakers of regional dialect at 313 localities spread over the whole of England. By the end of this year, all this basic material, if not actually published, will at least be available in proof, and thus easy to handle.[1] Our problem is how to present it with the maximum effectiveness and simplicity on maps. A specimen page[2] from one of our books of Basic Material is appended to show how the material appears in print.

As will be seen from the specimen page below (Figure 1), the individual items are all set out in the same way. First comes the number of the locality, then the response or responses. The entry often includes additional examples of the response form recorded incidentally from the informant's conversation during the interview

---

[1] *Survey of English Dialects,* ed. Harold Orton and Eugen Dieth.✝ (Leeds: E. J. Arnold and Son [publ. for the University of Leeds], 1962-   ). The *Introduction* and twelve books of Basic Material are now in print, thus completing the first stage of this series. [H.O., Oct. 1, 1971.]

[2] *Ibid.,* Vol. IV, Part 2, VI.13.9 HUNGRY.

with the fieldworker and occasionally from some comment about the response. This additional material provides invaluable confirmatory or supplementary evidence. Sometimes, indeed, it even corrects the actual response.

Thus the editors of the Linguistic Atlas have not only 313 × 1300 actual responses to deal with, but also the additional information recorded incidentally. This material would have been still bulkier if the Dieth-Orton Questionaire[3] had included more of the notions from the American questionaire[4] for the Linguistic Atlas of the United States and Canada. Their exclusion has probably deprived us of much important comparable material. However, we have an abundance of basic material available for mapping. Here are some figures, though not quite typical, giving the totals of certain words elicited by particular questions in our Questionaire. Most of them are synonyms, not simply phonetic variants: LEFT-HANDED 88; STRAWYARD (shelter plus farmyard where young cattle are sheltered, kept warm and fed during winter) 40; MID-MORNING-SNACK 40; WEAKEST MEMBER OF LITTER OF PIGS 72; SCRAPS (from pig's fat when rendered) 46; COWHOUSE 33; CHARLOCK 23. All our notions were not equally productive: some of the phonological questions understandably elicited only one response. With all this wealth of synonyms for individual notions available, the editor's problem is how to present the material most advantageously on maps. How can you put, say, fifty or more words clearly on a small map? It is indeed a problem.

In principle, there are two main types of linguistic maps. One is factual and non-interpretive; it shows all the material relating to a single notion overprinted on a map in phonetic transcription, e.g. L.A.N.E. In contrast, the second type is essentially interpretive. It displays the responses so as to reveal contrast, contrasts of linguistic and historical significance. These may be exhibited either by symbols, or else by isoglosses marking off distributional areas, which are then labelled clearly. Harold Allen's material presents

---

[3]*Ibid., Introduction,* pp. 40–113.

[4]*Handbood of the Linguistic Geography of New England,* ed. Hans Kurath, (Providence, Rhode Island: Brown University, 1939), pp. 150–158.

special problems and he has obviously developed a striking method of dealing with them.

Some factual atlases, for example the *Linguistic Atlas of New England,* have been beautifully executed. Nevertheless for myself, after much experimentation with maps that attempted to display all the responses to one notion on a single map—devising eighty different symbols can be quite a diversion—I am by now a firm believer in the "Interpretive Atlas." Consequently, I have put forward proposals below for an interpretive, small-sized, simple, clear, and inexpensive atlas, one that must not be beyond the pocket of the private individual, the scholar, the teacher, the student, or the interested amateur. It may be noted here that our printed books of basic material serve all the purposes of the factual atlas.[5] Further, they enable the mapper to make his maps without first having to copy the phonetic transcriptions onto separate sheets. Anyone who has worked from a factual atlas will know how tedious this task can be.

My scheme for a *Linguistic Atlas of England* proposes:

1. An open-ended publication, one unrestricted by book dimensions, but consisting of loose sheets of foolscap size, or smaller like those appended, that can be added to, map by map, until all the material is fully interpreted.

2. The maps to be black on white, not multi-colored.

3. A basic map showing an outline of England, plus, perhaps, Wales, and southernmost Scotland, and faint but clear dots indicating the geographical position of the localities in the Network.

4. The maps to be interpretive and isoglossic, with the areas of distribution clearly labelled, and with minimal explanatory legends, so reducing the cost of preparation.

5. The maps to be inexpensively produced, cheap enough to be regarded as expendable, and thus replaceable.

6. The maps to be published in folders or wallets, 100 at a time.

7. The maps to be classified in four linguistic categories, viz. lexical, phonological, morphological and syntactical, and numbered consecutively within these categories. For example, 1.410,

---

[5]Professor E. Kolb in his *Linguistic Atlas of England: Phonology of the Six Northern Counties* (Bern, 1967) has evidently failed to appreciate this point.

2.75, 3.83 and 4.31, the first figure being the number of the linguistic category concerned, the other figures being the number of the map within the category. On reconsideration, probably L. 410, P. 75, M. 83, S. 31 would be preferable references. The letters L, P, M, and S represent respectively lexical, phonological, morphological, and syntactical. [H.O., Oct. 1, 1971.]

8. All the maps relating to one notion to be issued together, yet to be classified in their appropriate linguistic category.

9. The top sheet of the series of maps relating to a particular notion to show a list of all the usages concerned, with, where available, word etymologies and dates of first occurrence; and, also, to indicate which of the items have been mapped. A specimen "top-sheet" referring to LEFT-HANDED is included below (Figure 2).

10. A stiffish polythene overlay map, to be provided for showing (a) county boundaries, (b) county numbers as used in our system,[6] (c) locality numbers, (d) main rivers, (e) contours above, say, 300 or 400 feet, and perhaps (f) three or four principal cities that would facilitate orientation.

We now come to the specific task of the editor. With his list of etymologised and dated occurrences in front of him—I am thinking of words in particular— the editor would now:

1. Decide which items, in point of etymology, recorded occurrence, or phonetic differentiation, could be significantly contrasted on maps, and which of these responses should appear on the same map. The basic material would thus be broken down into maps showing genuinely contrastive features.

2. Ensure that the individual maps do not display too many items, so avoiding clutter and obscurity.

Though I have not so far mentioned the possible use of the computer in our editorial arrangements, the question has been most seriously considered. Up to the present, and because of the lack of funds, a programmer, and additional philological assistance, we have been forced to delay our decision. Though utterly convinced of the urgent need for computerizing our Basic Material, and more so than ever after what Professor Wood has told us so impressively this morning, my Associate Editor, Mr. John Wid-

---

[6] *Survey of English Dialects*, Vol. I *(Introduction)*, p. 15, ¶ 1.4.

dowson,[7] and I intend to go ahead with our Linguistic Atlas immediately on my return to England, and while there is time. It seems to me essential to establish a satisfactory editorial procedure without further delay.

Finally, the following mapping conventions seem practicable and relevant.

1. Each locality dot in a "Labelled Area" is to be assumed to signify the occurrence there of the labelled item. This would be a novelty.

2. Where there is no occurrence of the labelled item at a particular locality, the dot concerned is to be encircled by a ring of cancellation in order to denote non-occurrence or, more accurately, that (for some reason or other) the expression did not emerge. Thus ⊙.

3. When the labelled item does not occur at a particular locality but is replaced by some other word, the locality dot concerned is to be encircled with a ring of cancellation and, in addition, a special symbol denoting the intruder is to be placed round the ring of cancellation. Thus ⊖. But the composite symbol seems to become clearer by omitting the base of the triangle. Thus ⟁.

4. When a second item occurs concurrently with the labelled item, the locality dot involved is to be enclosed by a separate symbol denoting this additional item. Thus △ or ⋀.

5. When a third item occurs at a particular locality—a rare feature—a separate symbol denoting this item is to be placed to the left of the enclosed locality dot. Thus □△ or ⊓⋀.

6. For mapping purposes no distinction in point of occurrence need be made between the actual response and an additional example from the incidental information. Both are of equal significance.

7. An outlier, stray or deviant that occurs in a non-labelled area may be shown by placing its symbol so that the top centre just covers the locality dot.

8. The space below the map may be used for drawing attention to any significant matter relating to the map, e.g., a deviant not taken into account on the map, the occurrence of a singular form instead of the wanted plural, etc. See, e.g., Figures 3, 9, 16.

---

[7] Lecturer in English, University of Sheffield.

9. On occasion the expressions relating to a synonym for a particular keyword emerge so unevenly over the network of localities that it will seem advantageous to reproduce them on a separate map all by themselves. In this case the mapping conventions referring to a "labelled area" would obviously be irrelevant. See Figure 14. See also Figure 17 for the distribution of a single synonym.

In working out these proposals, I have had in mind chiefly lexical items. But the procedures can be applied equally well to the other grammatical categories. One final point, however, should be emphasized, namely that we intend to use the simplest possible methods of interpreting the Basic Material, and to avoid cluttering our maps with detail.

The appended Figures illustrate the procedures outlined above. Figure 26 shows the network of localities investigated. The phonetic symbols and diacritics employed are as approved by the International Phonetic Association.

Postscript.

Since preparing the above article, I have discussed with my collaborator Dr. Nathalia Wright the revised method of mapping that we are using in our forthcoming *Word Geography of England* (to be published by the Seminar Press, London) and append a specimen map (Figure 27). The word labels in the margins of the maps printed above have been replaced, in the distributional areas on the map itself, by arabic numerals referring to the appropriate items in the legend. Dr. Wright and I are most grateful to Dr. Hans Kurath for recommending this procedure to us.

H. O.
March 28, 1971

750

VI.13.9 HUNGRY

Q. If you haven't eaten any food for a long time, you're bound to be very....

Rr. EMPTY, HOLLOW, HUNGERED, HUNGRY, LEAR(Y), PECKISH, SINKING, STARVED, STARVING, THIRL(Y)

31 So   1 ʌŋgɾi [ɫəɾi(2x) *leary* (n.d.)]   2 ʌŋgɾi, ɫəːː, °~   3 hʌŋgɾi   4 pɛkɪʃ [s.w. ɫəːː: *lear* (=*empty*)]   5 ɫəɾi   6 ʌŋgɾi, ɫəɾi [pref.]   7 ɫəɾi   8 ʌŋgəːːd, ɫəɾi, °ʌŋgəːːd   9 ɫəːːɾi, °~(2x)   10 ɫəːːɾi   11 li·əɾi   12 ɫəɾi, °hʌŋgəːːd³   13 ɫəɾi

32 W   1 ʌŋgɾi, ɫəːːɾi, °~   2 ʌŋgɾi, ɫəːː, °~   3 hʌŋgɾi, ɫəːː, °~   4 ɫəːː, °stəːːvɪn   5 ɫəːː, °~   6 ɫəːː   7 ʌŋgɾɪ   8 ɫəːː   9 ɫəːː, °~

33 Brk   1 ɫəːː   2 ɫəːː, °ʌŋgɹɪ⁴(2x)   3 ɫəɹ ["pref."], ɒŋgɹɪ, °ʌŋgɹɪ¹   4 ɫəɹ, °ʌŋgɹɪ   5 liəɹ

34 Sr   1 ɛmptɪ, s.w. ʌŋgɹɪ   2 ɫəɹ, °~   3 ʌŋgɹɪ, ɫəːː   4 ɫəːɾ [i.e. very hungry], °ʌŋgɹɪ   5 ɫəːː, hʌŋgɹɪ

35 K   1 ɒɲɹi   2 ʌŋgɹɪ, pɛkɪʃ   3 hɒŋgɹɪ   4 ʌŋgɹɪ   5–6 ɒŋgɹɪ   7 ʌŋgɹɪ, pɛkɪʃ

36 Co   1 ɫəːːɾi, °ðʌɾəɫ [esp. of cattle]   2 ɫəːːɾi, ðɛɾəɫ, °~   3 ɫəːːɾi, ðʌɾəɫ, °ɫəːːɾi   4 ɫəːːɾi, ʌŋgəːːd, ðəːːɾəɫ, °~, °ɫəːːɾi, °ʌŋgəːːd(2x)   5 ɫəːːɾi   6 ɫəːːɾi, θʌɾəɫ   7 ɫəːːɾi, °ðəːːʈi, °ʌŋgəːː¹ [*sic*]

37 D   1 ðəːːdʈ, °~   2 ɫəːːɾi, vəːːdʈ, °~   3 ɫəːːɾi, ðəːːdʈ   4–8 ɫəːːɾi   9 ɫəːːɾi, °ʌŋgɾi² [of animals]   10 ɫəːːɾi, °ʌŋgɾi²   11 ʌŋgəːːd, ɫəːːɾi, °ʌŋgəːːd

38 Do   1–2 ɫəɾi   3 ɫəɾɪ   4 ɫəɾɪ   5 ɫɛːɾɪ

39 Ha   1 ʌŋgɾi, ɫəːː, °~   2 ɫəɾi, °~   3 ɒɫəːː, ɫəːː, °~   4 ʌ̆·ɲɾɪ, °stəɾ·vd [i.e. very hungry]   5 ɫəːː, °~   6 ɫəːː   7 ɫəːɾ

40 Sx   1 sɪŋkɪn ["pref."], ɫəːɾ   2–3 ɫəːɾ   4 ʌŋgɹɪ, ɫəɾ ["older"], °~   5 ɫəːɾ ["older... rare"], ʌŋgɹɪ   6 ɫəːɾ

VI.13.10 THIRSTY*

Q. If you haven't drunk anything for a long time, you're bound to be very....

Rr. (A-)DRY, THIRSTY

Note—For additional exs. of DRY, see VII.6.19 (and refs.).

Fig. 1

LINGUISTIC ATLAS OF ENGLAND
LEFT-HANDED VI.7.13

Q. *Of a man who does everything with this (show your left hand), you say he is. . . .*

Rr. BACK-HANDED[M] f. BACK (OE *bæc*) *adv.* + HAND (OE *hand*) + -ED (see OED). ? Ref. clumsiness.

BALLOCK-HANDED ? f. BALLOCK 'testicle' + HANDED (*supra*). ? Abusive.

BANG-HAND(-ED) ? f. BANG (? fr. Scand.) *v.* 'thump' + HAND(ED) (*supra*). ? Ref. clumsiness.

BAWKY-HANDED ? f. BALLOCK (*supra*) + -Y (OE -*ig*) + HANDED (*supra*). ? Abusive.

BUCK-FISTED ? f. BUCK (OE *bucc*) 'male animal' + FIST (OE *fȳst*) + -ED (*supra*). ? Ref. clumsiness.

CACK-HANDED[M] f. CACK (? OE *cacc*) 'human excreta' + HANDED (*supra*). ? Abusive.

CACKY f. CACK (*supra*) + -Y (*supra, sub* BAWKY-HANDED). ? Abusive.

CAGGY[M] ? var. of CACKY (*supra*).

CAGGY-FISTED/HANDED f. CAGGY (*supra*) + resp. FISTED (*supra*) and HANDED (*supra*). ? abusive.

CAM-HANDED f. CAM (cf. Welsh *cam* 'crooked', 1st rec. 1600) + HANDED (*supra*). ? Ref. clumsiness.

CAR-HANDED/PAWED[M] f. CAR (cf. Gaelic *cearr*

Fig. 2

'left-handed, awkward') + resp. HANDED (*supra*) and PAWED fr. PAW (ME *pawe*) + -ED (*supra*).

CAT-HANDED f. CACK (*supra;* but see CAT-HANDED sub CAT *sb.*¹, EDD) + HANDED (*supra*).

CAWK-FISTED/HANDED ? var. of ĢAWK (but cf. CAWKING 'awkward', EDD) + resp. FISTED (*supra*) and HANDED (*supra*).

CAWKY f. CAWK (*supra*) + -Y (*supra*). But cf. CORKEY, EDD.

CAWKY-HANDED f. CAWKY (*supra*) + HANDED (*supra*).

CLICK^M cf. old Cornish *glikinindorn glikin* 'left-handed', EDD. Not rec. independently.

CLICKY^M f. CLICK (*supra*) + -Y (*supra*).

CLICKY-HANDED^M f. CLICKY (*supra*) + HANDED (*supra*).

COB-HANDED ? f. COB *v.* 'thump' + HANDED (*supra*). ? Ref. clumsiness.

COCK-FISTED ? f. CAWK (*supra*) by shortening + FISTED (*supra*).

COOCHY-GAMMY/HANDED/PAWED^M f. COOCHY *adj.* (q.v., EDD) + resp. GAMMY (*infra*), HANDED (*supra*), and PAWED (*supra*).

COW-HANDED/PAWED ? alteration of CAR (*supra*) + resp. HANDED (*supra*) and PAWED (*supra*).

Fig. 2 (cont.)

COWEY-HANDED   f. COW (*supra*) + -Y (*supra*) + HANDED (*supra*).

COWLY-HANDED   ? var. of COWEY (*supra*) + HANDED (*supra*).

CUDDY-HANDED[M] f. CUDDY 'donkey' (1st rec. c.1710), pet form of CUTHBERT, + HANDED (*supra*). ? Derisory.

CUNNY-HANDED   ? fr. CUNNY (see Partridge, *Dict. of Slang*, s.v.) + HANDED (*supra*). ? Abusive.

DOLL-PAWED   ? reduction of DOLLY, a blend of GOLLY (*infra*) + DOLL 'hand' (on which see EDD, s.v.) + PAWED (*supra*).

DOLLOCK-HANDED   ? blend of DOLL (*supra*) + -Y (*supra*) and GALLOCK (*infra*), + HANDED (*supra*).

DOLLY-PAWED   ? blend of DOLL (*supra*) and GOLLY (*supra*), + PAWED (*supra*).

GALLOCK-HANDED   f. GALLOCK (see GALLOCK HAND 'left hand', 1st rec. 1703, sub. GAWK *adj.* 'awkward', OED) + HANDED (*supra*).

GALLY-HANDED   ? var. of GALLOCK (*supra*) + HANDED (*supra*).

GAMMY-FISTED/HANDED[M]   f. GAMMY 'lame', 1st rec. 1879 OED, + resp. FISTED (*supra*) and HANDED (*supra*).

GAWK-HANDED   f. GAWK (see GALLOCK *supra*) + HANDED (*supra*).

Fig. 2 (cont.)

GAWKY-HANDED f. GAWK (*supra*) + -Y (*supra*) + HANDED (*supra*).

GAWP-HANDED ? alteration of GAWK (*supra*) + HANDED (*supra*).

GIBBLE-FISTED

GOLLY-HANDED ? var. of GALLY (*supra*) + HANDED (*supra*).

KAY-FIST(ED)/NEIVED/PAWED[M] f. KAY (1st rec. 13.. , OED) fr. Da. *kei* 'left' + resp. FIST(ED) (*supra*), NEIVE (ON *hnefi*, OED) and PAWED (*supra*). KAY-FISTED, KAY-NEIVED and KAY-PAWED 1st rec. resp. 1611, 1685 and 1895, OED.

KECK-FISTED/HANDED[M] ? f. var. of CACK (*supra*) + resp. FISTED (*supra*) and HANDED (*supra*). Derogatory.

KECKY-FISTED/HANDED ? f. KECK (*supra*) + -Y (*supra*) + resp. FISTED (*supra*) and HANDED (*supra*).

KEG-HANDED/PAWED ? f. var. of CAG (*supra*) + resp. HANDED (*supra*) and PAWED (*supra*).

KEGGY(-HANDED)[M] ? var. of CAGGY (*supra*) + HANDED (*supra*).

KITTAGH-HANDED f. Irish *ciotagh* 'left-handed' cf. EDD, + HAND (*supra*).

KITTAGHY see KITTAGH- (*supra*).

LEFT-CAGGY f. LEFT + CAGGY (*supra*).

Fig. 2 (cont.)

LEFT-COOCH(ED)   see COOCH(E), EDD.

LEFT-HAND(ED)^M f. LEFT (OE *left*) + HAND(ED) (*supra*).

LEFT-KEG(GED)/KELLY/PUG

MARLBOROUGH-HANDED   f. MARLBOROUGH (fr. name of Wiltshire village, the natives of which were traditionally famed for clumsiness, EDD) + HANDED (*supra*).

SCOOCHY   var. of COOCHY (*supra*).

NORTH-HANDED   Probably spurious.

SCRAM(MY)-HANDED   cf. SCRAM-HAND 'withered hand', EDD. ? Hence 'clumsy'.

SCROOCHY   var. of (S)COOCHY (*supra*).

SCRUMMY-HANDED

SKAY-PAWED   var. of KAY-PAWED (*supra*).

SKIFFY(-HANDED)

SKIVVY-HANDED   var. of SKIFFY-HANDED (*supra*).

SOUTH-PAWED   f. SOUTH (OE *sūþ*) + PAWED (*supra*), fr. Amer. Engl. SOUTH-PAW 'left-hander'.

SQUIFFY   ? var. of SKIFFY (*supra*).

SQUIPPY   ? corruption of SKIFFY (*supra*).

Fig. 2 (cont.)

SQUIVVER-HANDED ? var. of SKIVVY-HANDED (*supra*).

WATTED cf. WATTY 'simpleton', EDD. ? Derisory.

WATTY(-HANDED)^M f. WATTY (supra) + HANDED (*supra*).

Fig. 2 (cont.)

LINGUISTIC ATLAS OF ENGLAND

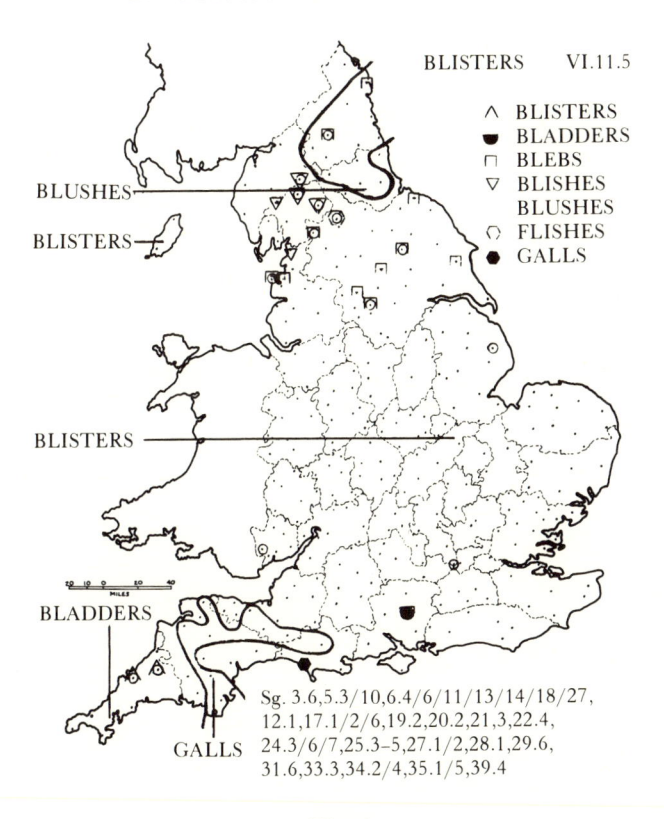

BLISTERS   VI.11.5

∧ BLISTERS
● BLADDERS
⊓ BLEBS
▽ BLISHES
  BLUSHES
⌒ FLISHES
● GALLS

BLUSHES
BLISTERS
BLISTERS
BLADDERS
GALLS

Sg. 3.6,5.3/10,6.4/6/11/13/14/18/27, 12.1,17.1/2/6,19.2,20.2,21,3,22.4, 24.3/6/7,25.3–5,27.1/2,28.1,29.6, 31.6,33.3,34.2/4,35.1/5,39.4

Fig. 3

LINGUISTIC ATLAS OF ENGLAND

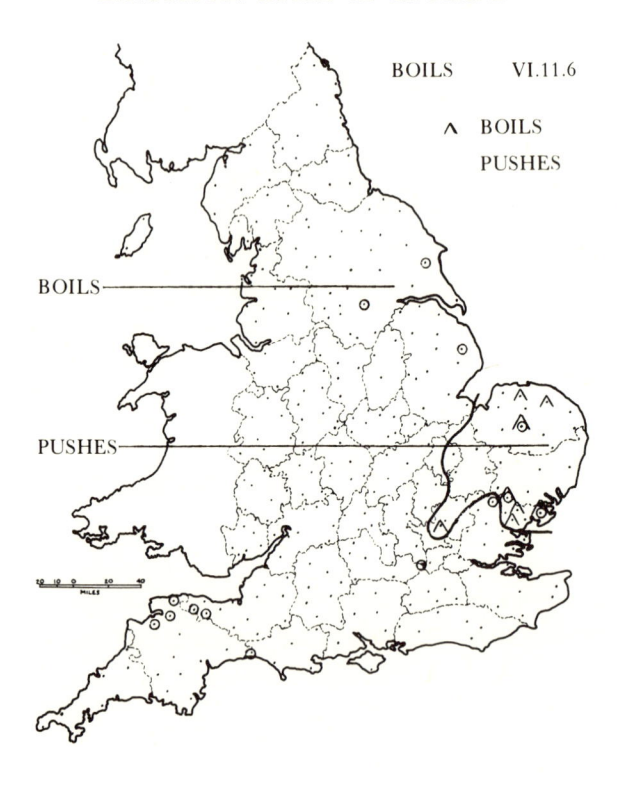

BOILS VI.11.6

∧ BOILS
PUSHES

BOILS

PUSHES

Fig. 4

LINGUISTIC ATLAS OF ENGLAND

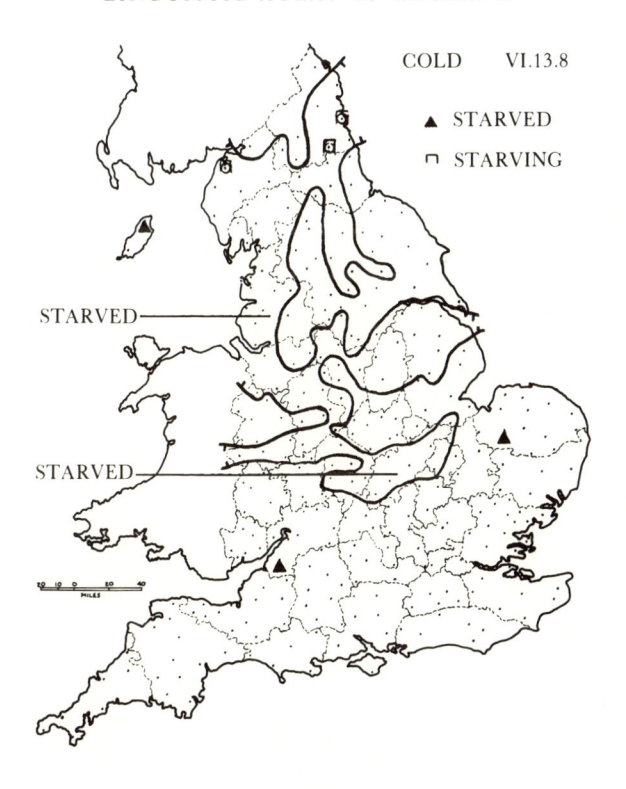

COLD   VI.13.8

▲ STARVED
⊓ STARVING

STARVED

STARVED

Fig. 5

LINGUISTIC ATLAS OF ENGLAND

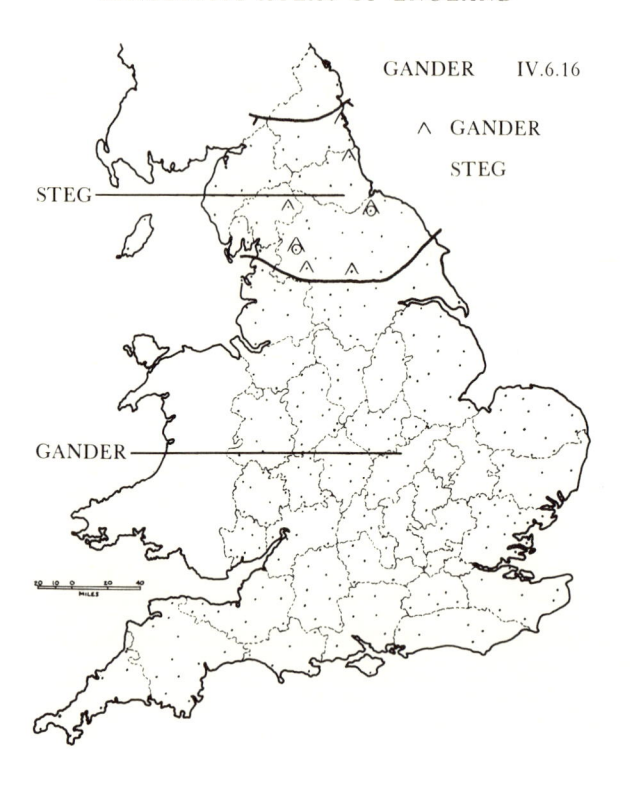

GANDER   IV.6.16

∧ GANDER
    STEG

STEG

GANDER

Fig. 6

LINGUISTIC ATLAS OF ENGLAND

GRINDSTONE IV.2.7

▲ GRINDSTONE

GRINDSTONE

GRINDSTONE

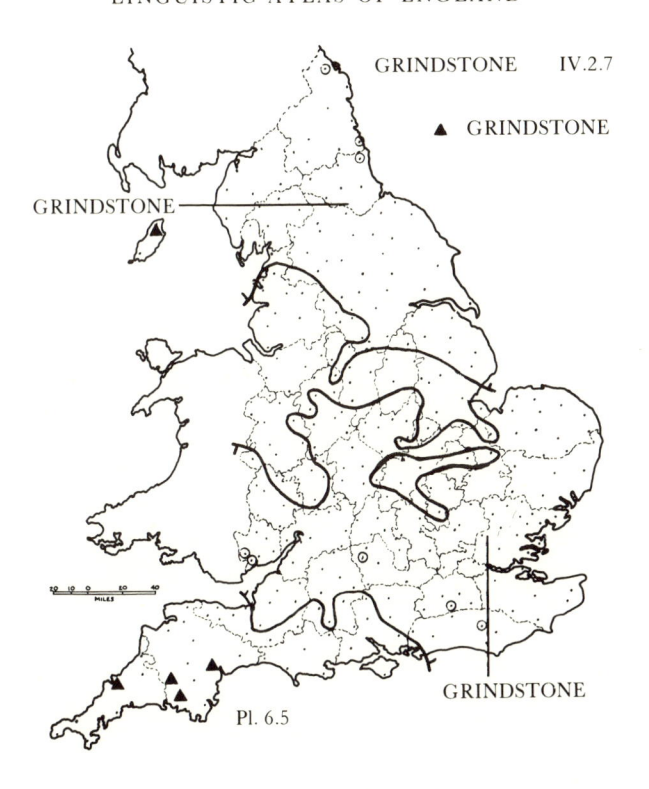

Pl. 6.5

Fig. 7

LINGUISTIC ATLAS OF ENGLAND

GRINDSTONE IV.2.7
▫ GRINDING-STONE
GRINDLE-STONE

GRINDLE-STONE

GRINDING-STONE

GRINDLE-STONE

GRINDING-STONE

Fig. 8

LINGUISTIC ATLAS OF ENGLAND

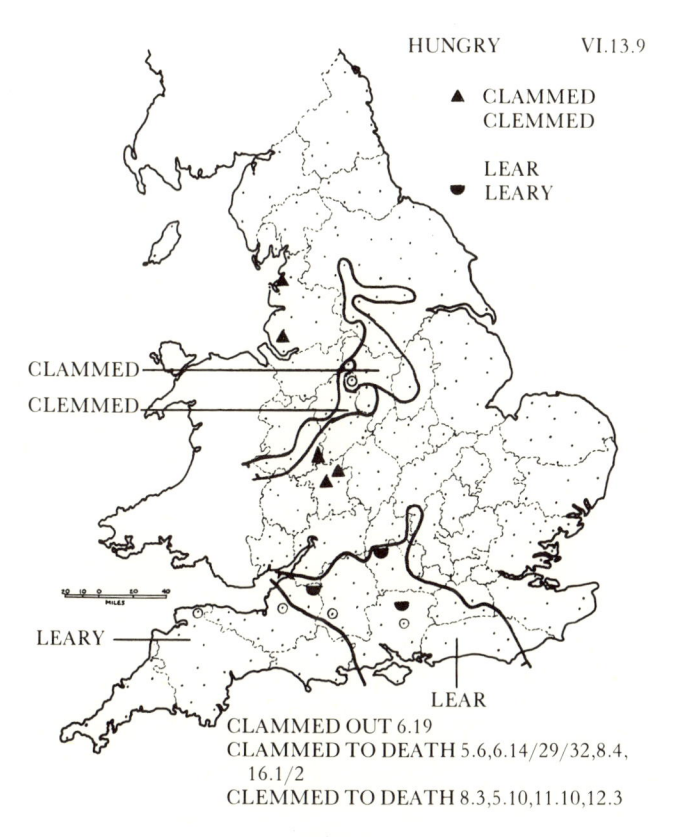

HUNGRY VI.13.9

▲ CLAMMED
  CLEMMED

  LEAR
◖ LEARY

CLAMMED
CLEMMED

LEARY

LEAR

CLAMMED OUT 6.19
CLAMMED TO DEATH 5.6,6.14/29/32,8.4,
   16.1/2
CLEMMED TO DEATH 8.3,5.10,11.10,12.3

Fig. 9

LINGUISTIC ATLAS OF ENGLAND

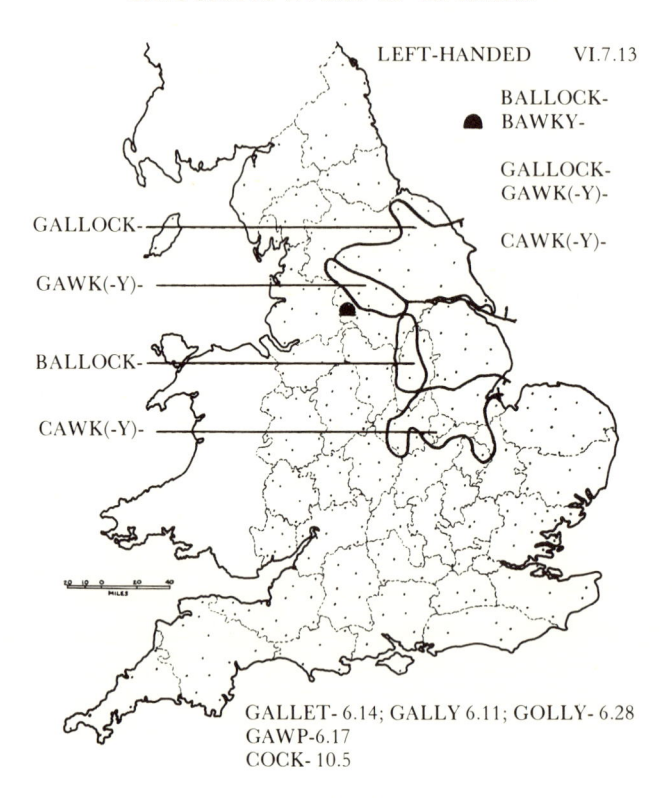

LEFT-HANDED   VI.7.13
BALLOCK-
BAWKY-
GALLOCK-
GAWK(-Y)-
CAWK(-Y)-

GALLOCK-
GAWK(-Y)-
BALLOCK-
CAWK(-Y)-

GALLET- 6.14; GALLY 6.11; GOLLY- 6.28
GAWP-6.17
COCK- 10.5

Fig. 10

LINGUISTIC ATLAS OF ENGLAND

LEFT-HANDED VI.7.13

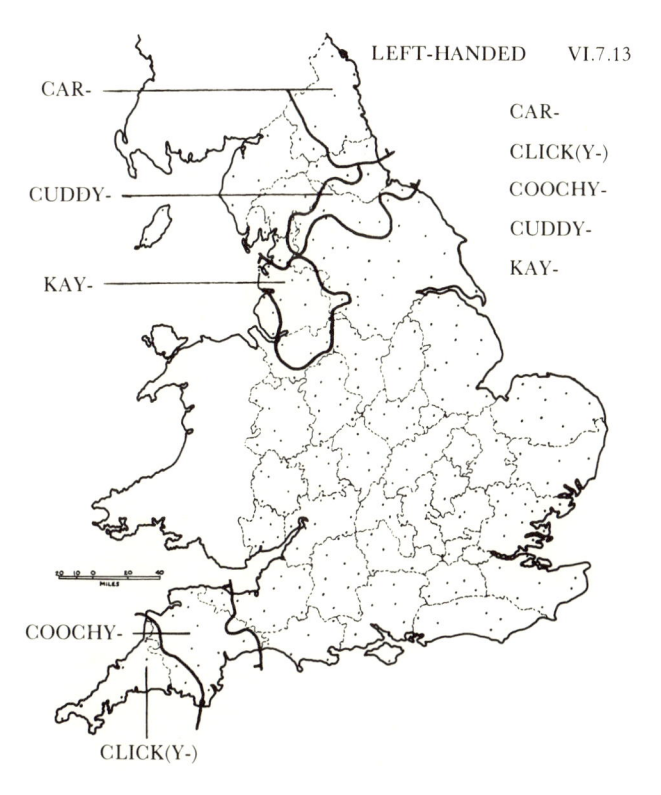

CAR-
CUDDY-
KAY-
COOCHY-
CLICK(Y-)

CAR-
CLICK(Y-)
COOCHY-
CUDDY-
KAY-

Fig. 11

LINGUISTIC ATLAS OF ENGLAND

LEFT-HANDED VI.7.13(a)

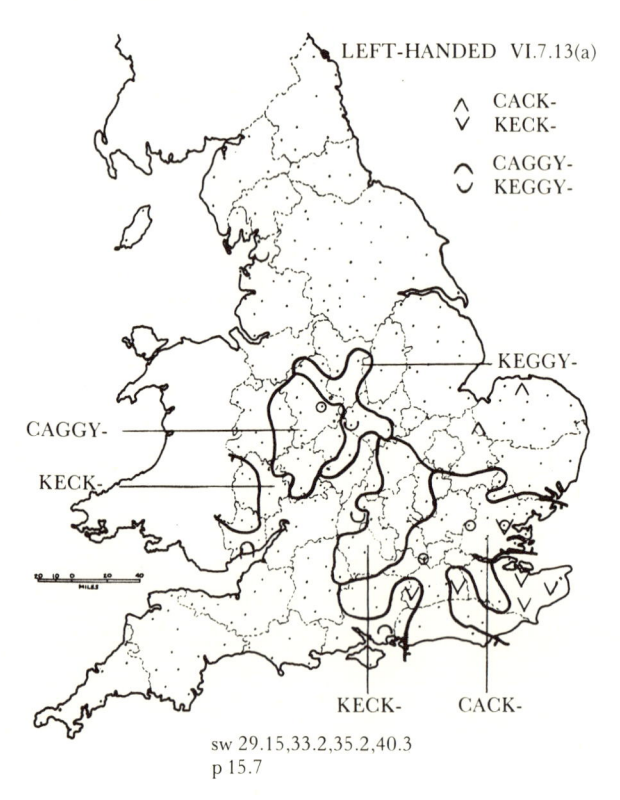

∧∨ CACK-
   KECK-

⌒⌣ CAGGY-
   KEGGY-

KEGGY-
CAGGY-
KECK-
KECK- CACK-

sw 29.15, 33.2, 35.2, 40.3
p 15.7

Fig. 12

LINGUISTIC ATLAS OF ENGLAND

LEFT-HANDED   VI.7.13

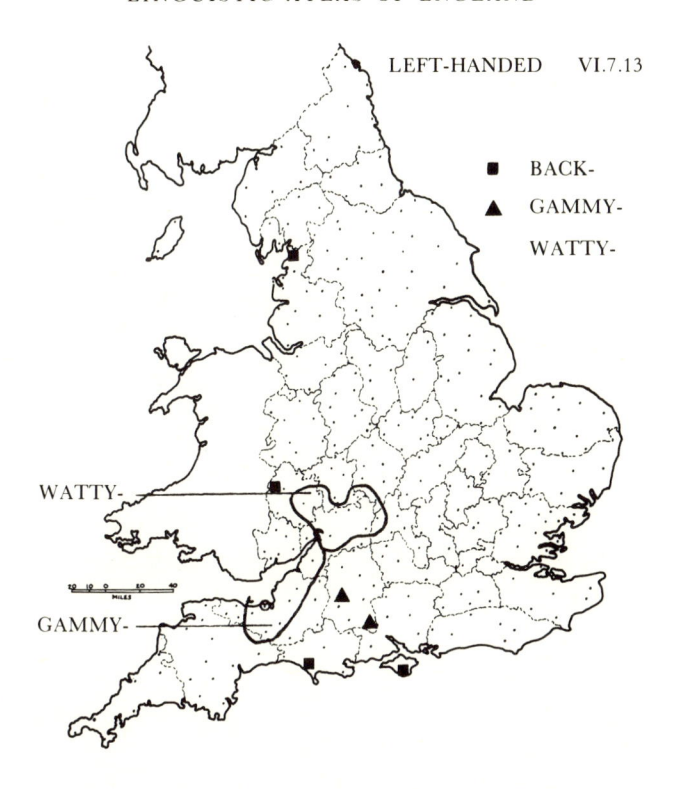

■ BACK-
▲ GAMMY-
   WATTY-

WATTY-

GAMMY-

Fig. 13

LINGUISTIC ATLAS OF ENGLAND

LEFT-HANDED   VI.7.13

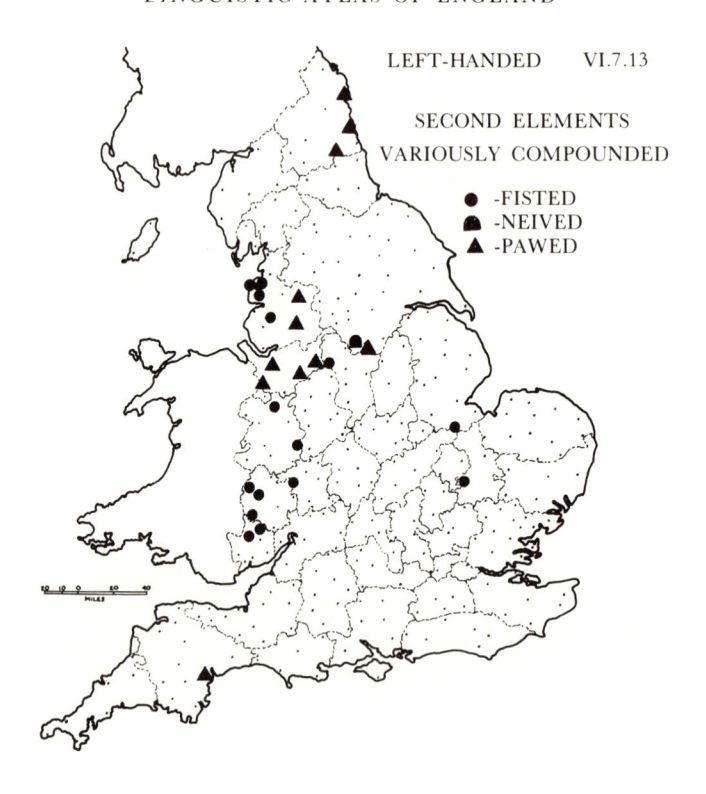

SECOND ELEMENTS
VARIOUSLY COMPOUNDED

● -FISTED
▲ -NEIVED
▲ -PAWED

Fig. 14

LINGUISTIC ATLAS OF ENGLAND

LEFT-HANDED   VI.7.13

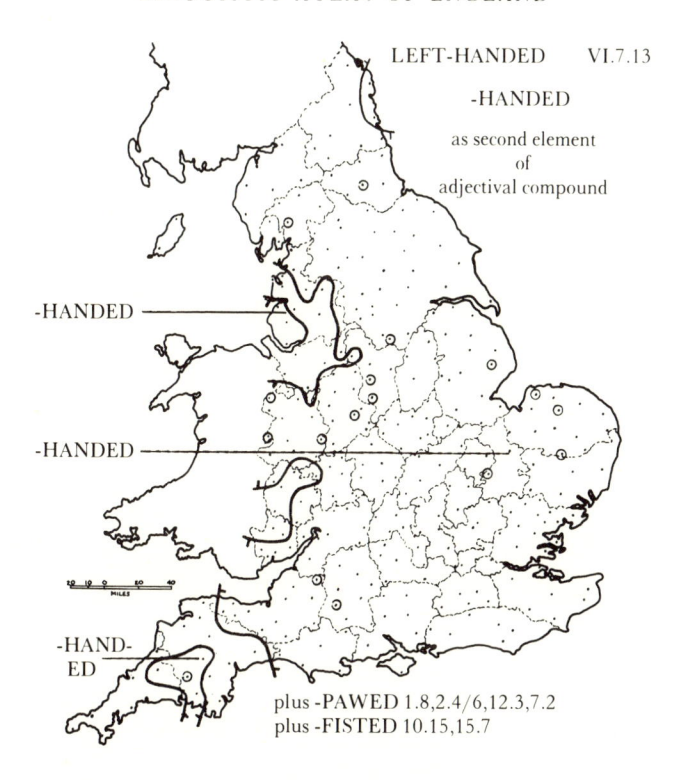

-HANDED

as second element of adjectival compound

-HANDED

-HANDED

-HAND-ED

plus -PAWED 1.8, 2.4/6, 12.3, 7.2
plus -FISTED 10.15, 15.7

Fig. 15

LINGUISTIC ATLAS OF ENGLAND

LEFT-HANDED   VI.7.13

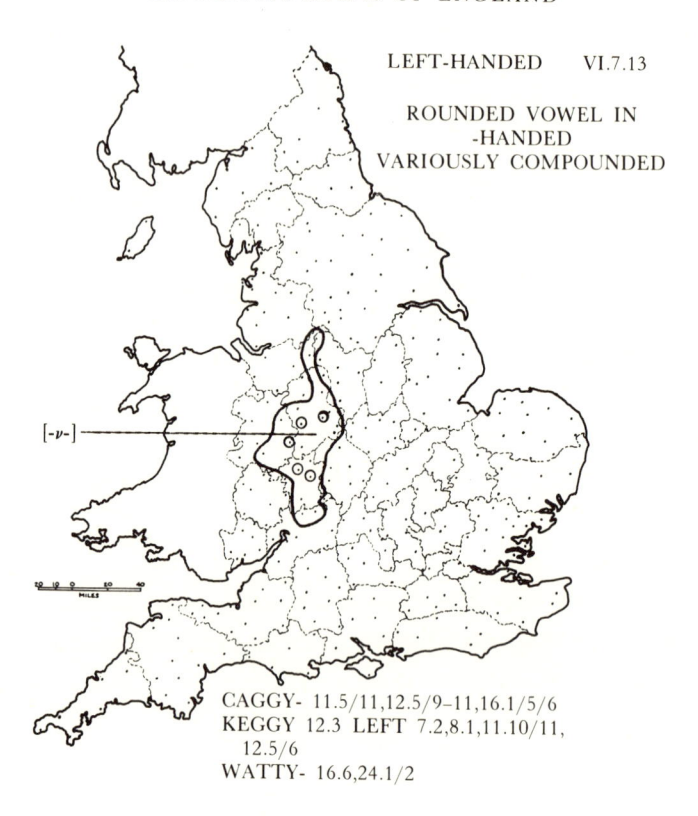

ROUNDED VOWEL IN -HANDED VARIOUSLY COMPOUNDED

[-ʋ-]

CAGGY- 11.5/11,12.5/9–11,16.1/5/6
KEGGY 12.3 LEFT 7.2,8.1,11.10/11, 12.5/6
WATTY- 16.6,24.1/2

Fig. 16

LINGUISTIC ATLAS OF ENGLAND

LEFT-HANDED VI.7.13

• LEFT-HANDED

Fig. 17

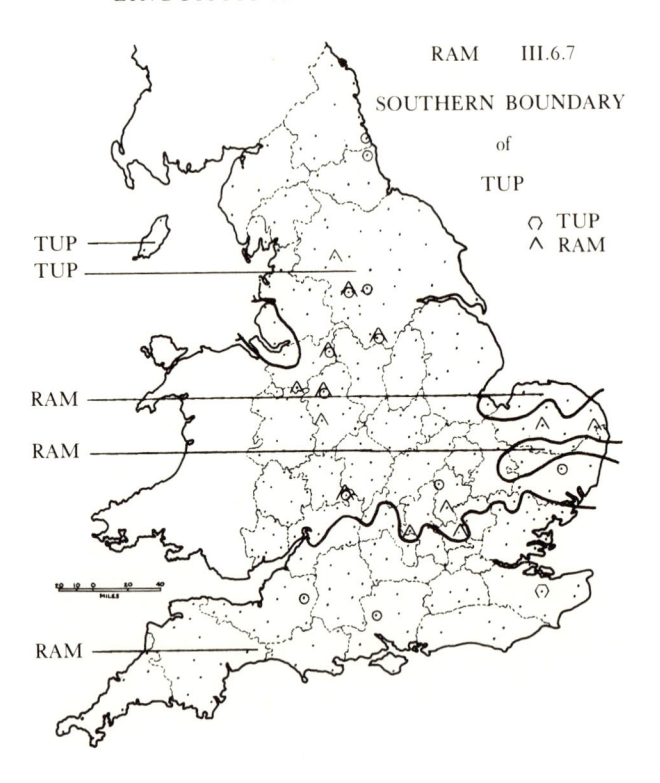

Fig. 18

LINGUISTIC ATLAS OF ENGLAND

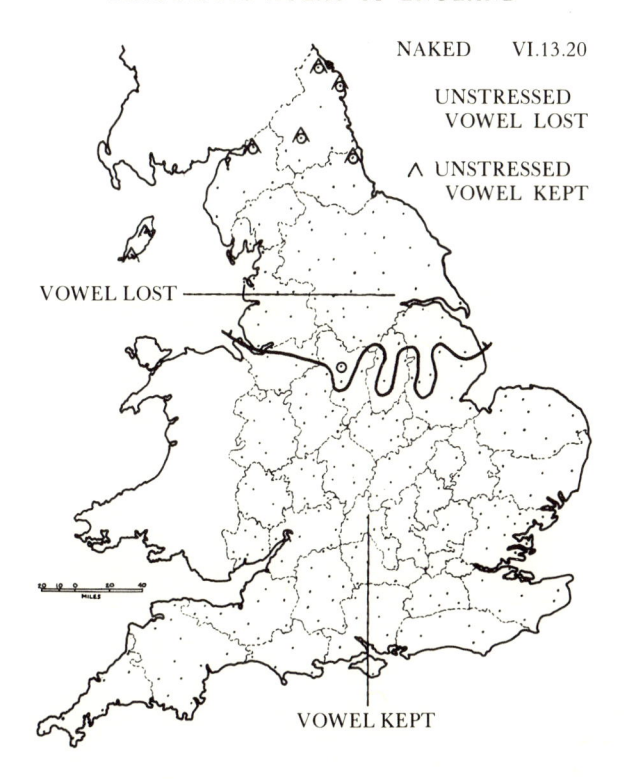

NAKED VI.13.20

UNSTRESSED VOWEL LOST

∧ UNSTRESSED VOWEL KEPT

VOWEL LOST

VOWEL KEPT

Fig. 19

108   Dialectology: Problems and Perspectives

LINGUISTIC ATLAS OF ENGLAND

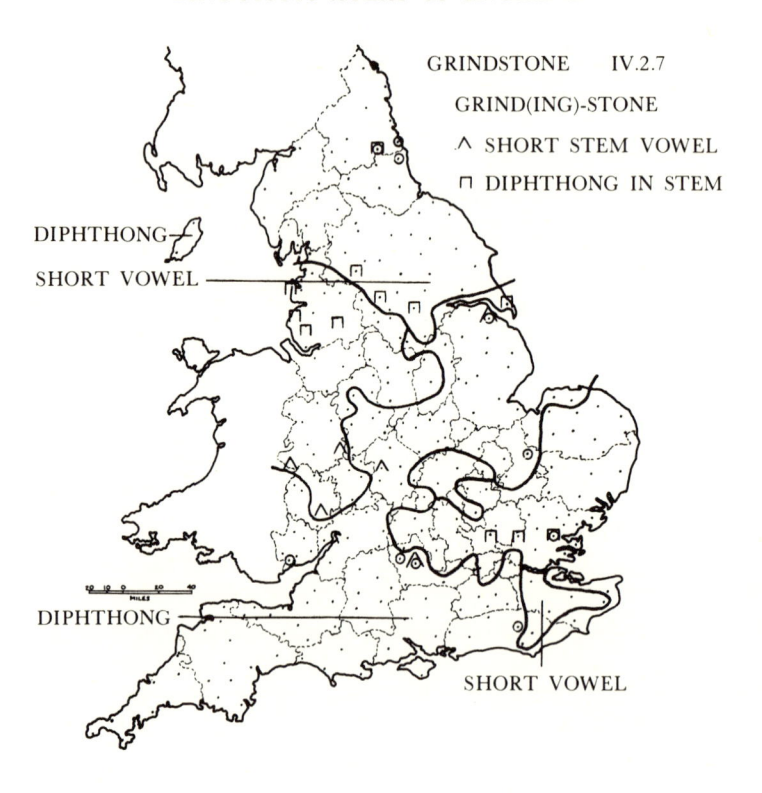

GRINDSTONE   IV.2.7
GRIND(ING)-STONE
∧ SHORT STEM VOWEL
⊓ DIPHTHONG IN STEM

DIPHTHONG
SHORT VOWEL

DIPHTHONG

SHORT VOWEL

Fig. 20

LINGUISTIC ATLAS OF ENGLAND

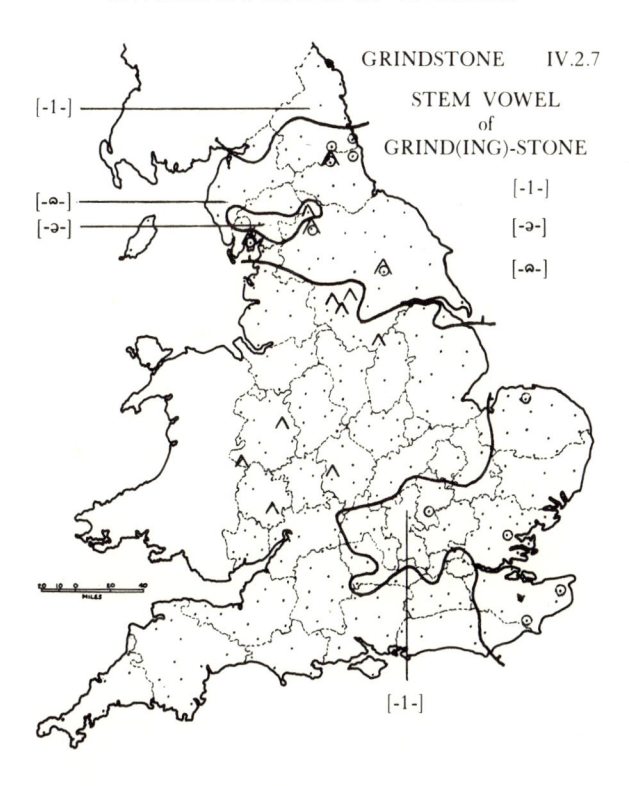

GRINDSTONE IV.2.7
STEM VOWEL
of
GRIND(ING)-STONE

[-ɪ-]
[-ə-]
[-ɑ-]

Fig. 21

LINGUISTIC ATLAS OF ENGLAND

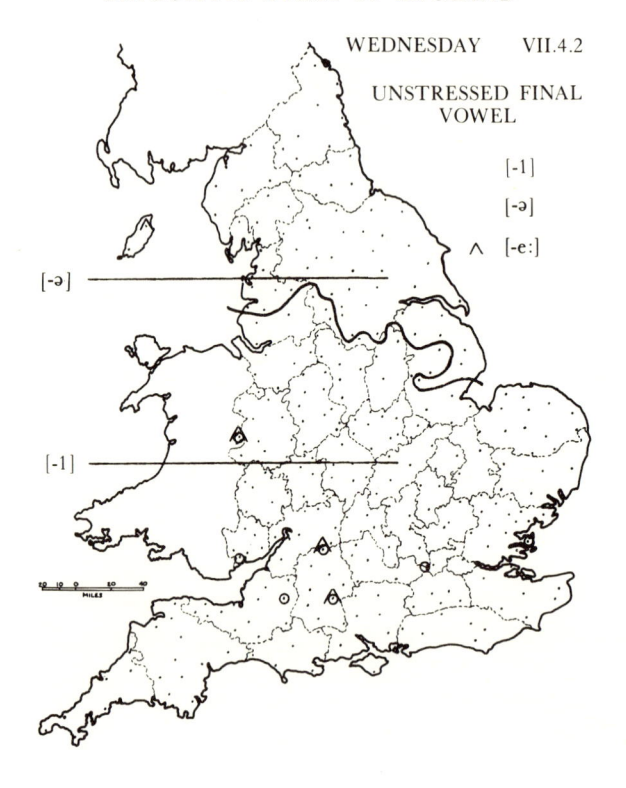

WEDNESDAY VII.4.2

UNSTRESSED FINAL VOWEL

[-ɪ]
[-ə]
∧ [-eː]

[-ə]

[-ɪ]

Fig. 22

LINGUISTIC ATLAS OF ENGLAND

LEFT-HANDED VI.7.13

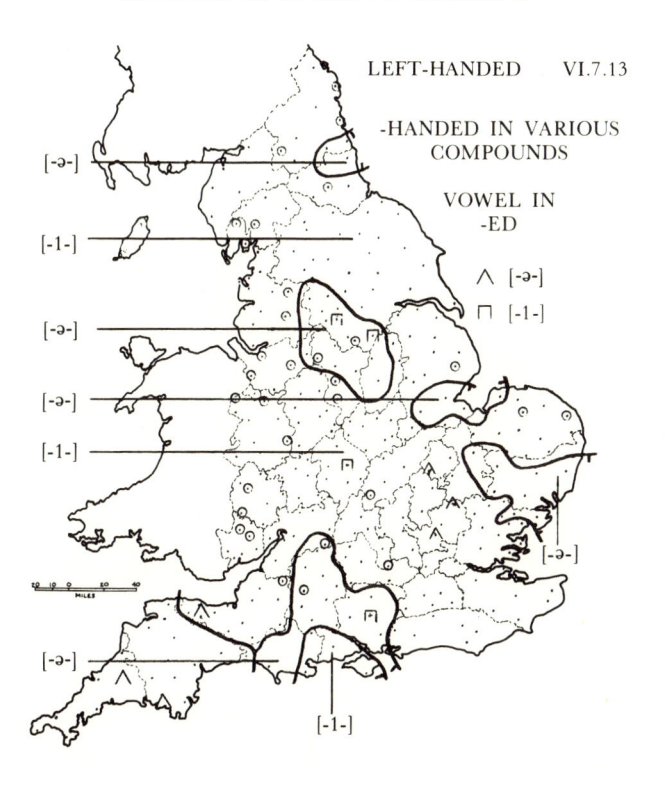

-HANDED IN VARIOUS COMPOUNDS

VOWEL IN -ED

∧ [-ə-]
⊓ [-1-]

Fig. 23

LINGUISTIC ATLAS OF ENGLAND

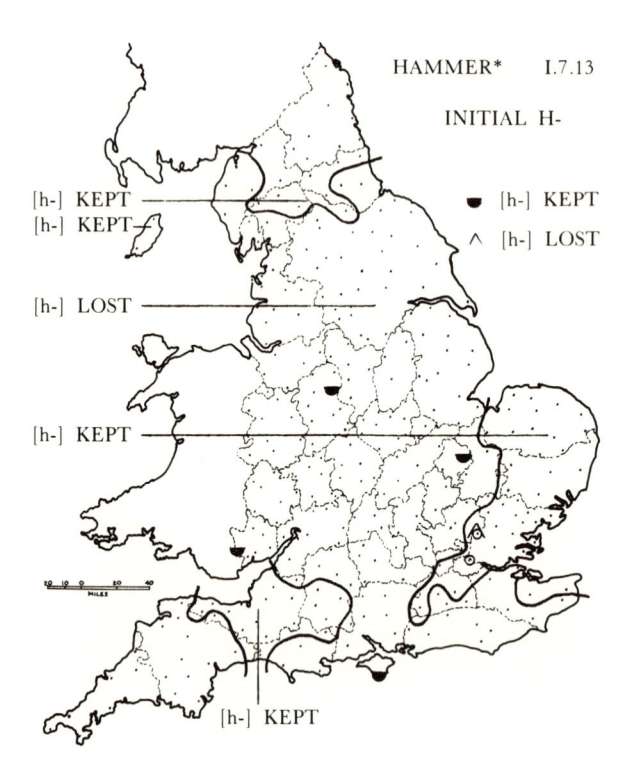

HAMMER* I.7.13

INITIAL H-

[h-] KEPT
[h-] KEPT
[h-] LOST
[h-] KEPT
[h-] KEPT

● [h-] KEPT
∧ [h-] LOST

Fig. 24

LINGUISTIC ATLAS OF ENGLAND

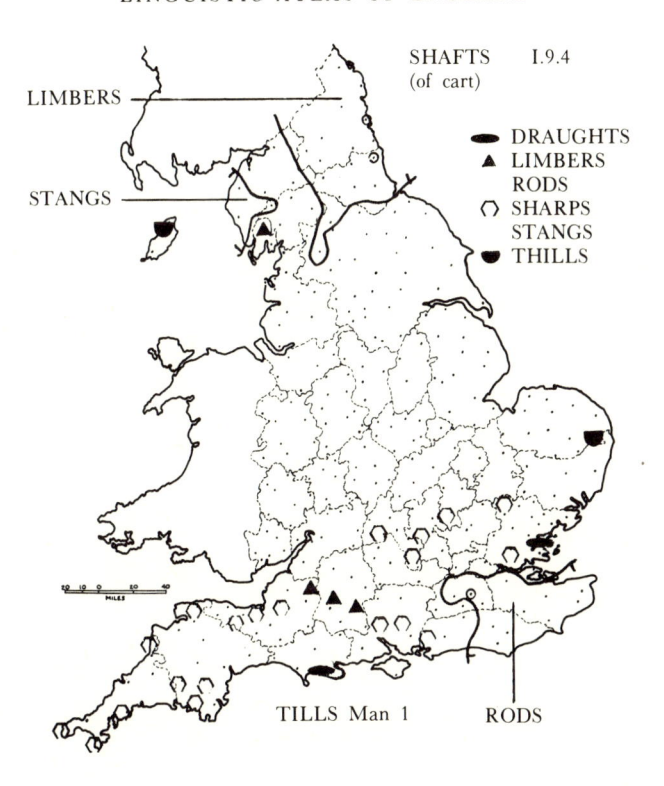

SHAFTS I.9.4
(of cart)

LIMBERS

STANGS

● DRAUGHTS
▲ LIMBERS
   RODS
⌂ SHARPS
   STANGS
▼ THILLS

TILLS Man 1   RODS

Fig. 25

114   Dialectology: Problems and Perspectives

LINGUISTIC ATLAS OF ENGLAND

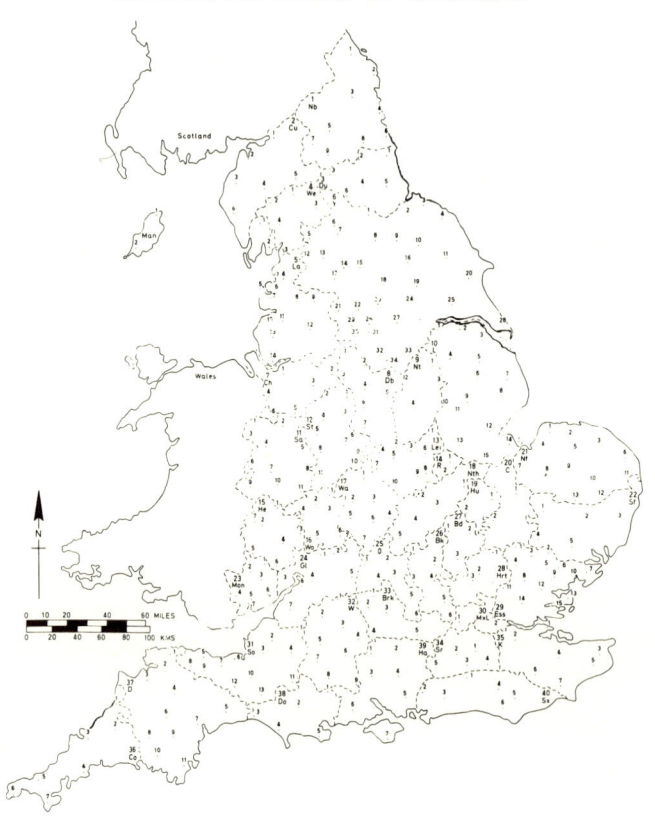

Fig. 26

LINGUISTIC ATLAS OF ENGLAND

GRINDSTONE IV.2.7

What do you call that big round thing which you turn to sharpen your tools on?

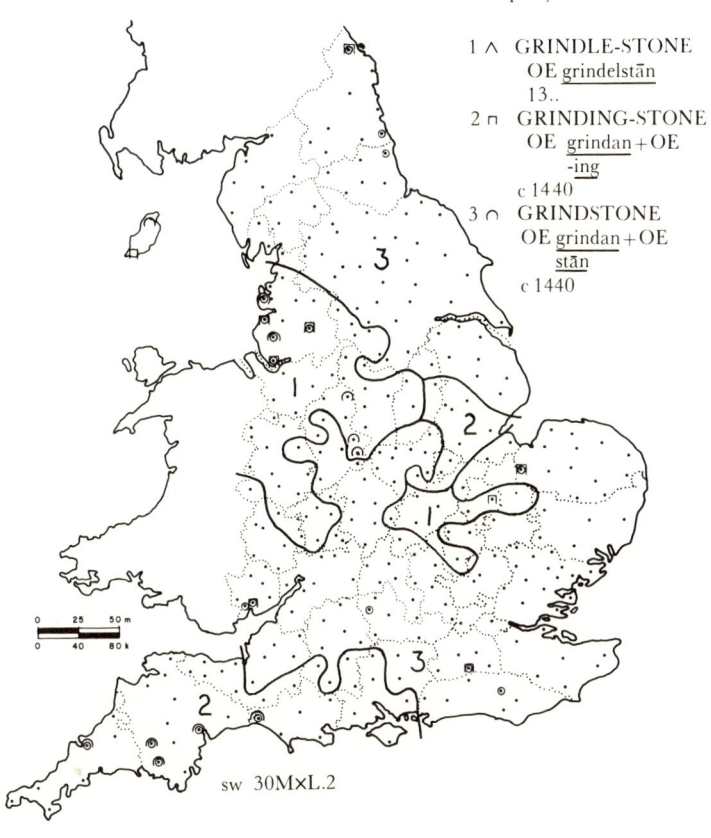

1 ∧ GRINDLE-STONE
     OE grindelstān
     13..
2 ⊓ GRINDING-STONE
     OE grindan + OE
        -ing
     c 1440
3 ⌒ GRINDSTONE
     OE grindan + OE
        stān
     c 1440

sw 30M×L.2

Fig. 27

Part III

Fieldwork in the Southern United States

WHAT HAPPENS IN TENNESSEE?

Raven I. McDavid, Jr.

University of Chicago

It is important to ask what may happen in Tennessee, because when we undertake a new linguistic survey, it is imperative that we ask the right questions if we expect to get the right answers. Part of what I say, of course, is based on cultural information that is anybody's knowledge for the seeking, in encyclopedias and elsewhere. Part of it comes by extrapolation from field work that has previously been done, by myself and others, in the South and elsewhere; if a good deal of it comes from my own field work, it is simply easier for me to dredge up out of my subconscious some of the details, such as the fact that *range* was used in the South for common grazing land in the days before the law required that cattle be fenced in—nor does it hurt that I have the files for the Middle and South Atlantic States and the North-Central region accessible to me in my own office. A large measure of it, finally, comes from the well-programmed intuition of an ex-Southerner who has frequently crossed the state of Tennessee on various satanic peregrinations, and whose own cultural heritage makes him aware of the complexities of the speechways reflecting the folkways of a border state. And that I have in Knoxville old friends, students, and a charming daughter as our enterprise—a survey of the Gulf States—gets under way is simply another reason that the occasion is both challenging and inviting.

As the Linguistic Atlas of the Gulf States moves from dream to reality, one of the most interesting questions for it to answer is what happens in Tennessee to the patterns of distribution of linguistic features that have been regionally identified along the Atlantic Seaboard.

As matters now stand, Tennessee is the oldest English-speaking area in the United States as yet unsurveyed for a regional linguistic atlas. As the sixteenth state admitted to the Union, in 1796, it is senior to many states whose local speechways scholars have found worthy of systematic exploration. Iowa, the oldest state in Mr. Allen's happily completed survey,[1] is fifty years younger; in the North-Central States, where I have worked with Marckwardt since 1948,[2] only Kentucky is older, and that by a mere four years. On the Pacific Coast, we have full evidence from California and Nevada and part of Washington; in the Rockies, a complete survey of Colorado and much evidence from Idaho, Montana, Utah, New Mexico, and Arizona—all much younger than Tennessee.

The reasons for this lag are painfully familiar to those who understand the South. A good deal of it derives from endemic poverty, from the long commitment of the South to an agricultural economy, and to regional subservience as a domestic colony of Northern industry. A good deal of it comes from the fact that Southern institutions have not had the funds to support distinguished scholarship that demands both highly technical training and peculiar sensitivity to human values, in situations involving close interpersonal relationships. And part of it, perhaps, may be due to the fact that many Southerners prefer to sentimentalize their folk traditions when they might study them seriously. There has been much made of the romantic speech of our Appalachian kinsmen, with its Elizabethan or Chaucerian survivals, but little effort has been expended by Southern scholars to see how Appalachian speech-ways pattern with those of the rest of the United States, let alone of Britain. There has been a good deal of study of the Gullah Negroes of the South Carolina and Georgia coast, but little effort on the part of Southern scholars to investigate either the African backgrounds of Gullah or the relationships of this dialect to other American regional dialects or to the white speech of the same area, or in fact even of the same communities. It is a lamentable fact that this lack of effort has made it profitable for half-baked carpetbaggers to promote themselves as authorities on

---

[1] The first volumes of the *Linguistic Atlas of the Upper Midwest* (Minnesota, Iowa, Nebraska, the Dakotas), directed by Harold B. Allen of the University of Minnesota, are scheduled to appear in 1971.

[2] *The Linguistic Atlas of the North-Central States* (Wisconsin, Michigan, southwestern Ontario, Illinois, Indiana, Kentucky, Ohio) was launched in 1938 by Albert H. Marckwardt of the University of Michigan (later of Princeton); editing is under way.

some mythical entities which they have set up as a monolithic "black English," or even "child black English"—to use one of the most appalling syntactic monstrosities they have created.

The reluctance of Southern observers to come to grips, seriously and systematically, with Southern speechways and their affiliations can be documented by a score of anecdotes from my own field work, including the query of the ordinary in Milledgeville, Georgia—a functionary that in South Carolina would be called the judge of probate—"Isn't all that in *Gone with the Wind?*" But even greater rigidity has been shown by some of those whose training and experience entitle them to know better. A recent Ph.D. from Chicago, Charles-James M. Bailey—originally, I believe, from Middlesboro, Kentucky—has spent a lot of time trying to refute Kurath's well-documented case for a Midland dialect region, deriving from Pennsylvania and including much of the territory hitherto labeled as "Southern."[3] What is more, Bailey does not attempt to prove his case by the systematic examination of comparable and accessible data, collected by trained investigators in scores of communities, or by making his own collection and codification of data, but tries to do it by the kind of thaumaturgical prestidigitation, of so-called 'rules' and 'underlying forms', that has been inflicted on American education by the Lower Charles River hirelings of the military establishment. Leaving aside all theoretical and ideological issues, I rather suspect that Bailey simply wishes to be known as a Southern gentleman and feels that a Pennsylvania origin of the kind of English he talks would besmirch his cultural escutcheon. And this attitude characterizes many Southerners and South Midlanders, learned and unlearned alike.

Whether or not—or to what extent—the speech of the Interior South is derived from Pennsylvania or the Southern coastal region—and Kurath's *Word Geography,* to say nothing of Bagby Atwood's later studies, clearly states that the relationships are complex, with the South Midland a very complicated transition area[4]—the matter cannot be settled either by wit or by Chom-

---

[3] Mr. Bailey presented his argument at the summer meeting of the Linguistic Society of America, Champaign, Illinois, July 1968.

[4] Hans Kurath, *A Word Geography of the Eastern United States* (University of Michigan, Ann Arbor: Michigan Press, 1949).

skemic manipulations. It requires painstaking labor, in examining the demographic origins of the region and the cultural forces operating in it. The historical record of voting patterns within a state, to say nothing of the long tradition of conflict between upland yeoman and lowland planter, is worth far more than emotional attachment to "Southern tradition," ancestral acres (real or mythical) and lost causes.[5] But this kind of investigation takes scholars trained in linguistic disciplines, and the South—regrettably—has not produced them. Leaving out a few individuals who have produced distinguished local studies, such as James B. McMillan of Alabama and Juanita Williamson of LeMoyne, Memphis (both trained in the Middle West, though Southern born), we have as yet only the studies directed by C. M. Wise of L.S.U. and the gallant unfinished work of Bagby Atwood in Texas, as tokens of the kind of systematic field investigations needed in the interior South. Such centers of Southern scholarship as Duke and North Carolina and Vanderbilt have contributed to the early stages of this kind of work—the Linguistic Atlas of the Middle and South Atlantic States—only a token fellowship from Duke and Carolina to support the field work in North Carolina, field work conducted by an investigator trained at Wisconsin and London; and today, when the survey of the interior South gets under way, it derives much of its leadership from scholars trained at the University of Chicago.

But this, of course, is not without respectable precedent. Years ago Mencken noted that the Linguistic Atlas of the United States and Canada was organized by an Austrian-born philologist, with several other foreign ethnic strains prominent on his staff. Yet the Austrian-born philologist had been trained at Wisconsin-Milwaukee, Texas, and Chicago; and continuing the tradition, the Chicago-trained scholars involved in this new project have had some of their training from a sixth-generation Up-Country South Carolinian, who somehow manages to combine after hours such diverse rôles as a life member of the NAACP, the son of a lobbyist for the

---

[5]The sectional divisions on political issues are shown in V. O. Key, *Southern Politics in State and Nation* (New York, 1946). For linguistic patterns correlating with voting patterns, see Raven I. McDavid, Jr., "Postvocalic /-r/ in South Carolina: a Social Analysis," *American Speech*, 23 (1948), 195-204.

cement industry, and the grandson of one of the few authentic privates in the Confederate army.

Now in designing a working plan for the state of Tennessee, we must take into account several ineluctable facts. Here, of course, the one who presents a proposal can count on the superior counter-intuitions of natives to correct incidental mistakes.

Tennessee is a state of peculiar shape and size. It is barely 112 miles across at the widest point; yet by highway it is some 500 miles from east to west, from Mountain City to Memphis. It is cut into three traditional domains—East, Middle and West Tennessee—by the Cumberland Plateau and the red hills between the Tennessee and the Mississippi. The major rivers, the Tennessee and the Cumberland, rising in the Appalachians, swing southwest and then northwest, to enter the Ohio not far upstream from the confluence of the Ohio and the Mississippi. Even in the heyday of rail travel, it was very difficult to go by train from east to west within the state; the only such route from Knoxville to Nashville was the late Tennessee Central—sometimes affectionately called the "Tennessee Creeper"—with a slow schedule and beautiful scenery along most of its right of way. Clingman's Dome, in the Great Smoky range along the North Carolina line, reaches 6642 feet above sea level, while Memphis on the Mississippi is but 182. From colonial days on, East Tennessee has been strikingly different in outlook from the central and western parts of the state. The eastern counties never joined the Confederacy, and consistently voted Republican—at least in national elections—long before that action became respectable elsewhere in the South. The cotton country of West Tennessee was also often at odds with the tobacco and dairying interests of the Nashville Basin.[6] Under the benign dictatorship of the late E. H. Crump—who was not only the Maecenas of the blues but also gave the vote, in Memphis, to thousands of Mississippi Negroes before they could cast a ballot at home—Memphis often cast the decisive votes in statewide elections. Of the 1933 referendum on the repeal of national prohibition, Will Rogers remarked that the thirst of Memphians apparently was more powerful than the desire of East Tennesseans to

---

[6] At one time (and it may still be true), Middle Tennessee had the largest Jersey herds in the United States, if not in the entire world.

protect their local industry. The state has an extraordinary variety of agricultural and mineral resources, all of which will bear on the design of the questionnaire; Merrimon Cuninggim, now director of the Danforth Foundation, once remarked to me at Duke that Tennessee was probably the only state that had within its limits all the resources for a self-contained modern economy. There is no single dominant industry, despite the headlines for Oak Ridge and the TVA; in fact, as no out-of-stater need remind a Tennessee audience, the TVA has fostered a variegated industrial development, especially in light industry.

Unlike many of the Southern states, Tennessee was never dominated by the plantation system. On the eve of the War of Northern Aggression, as some of us call the late unpleasantness of the 1860s, the proportion of Negroes was about 22 percent; a century later it was 16 percent, giving for the state a total black population of no more than 570,000—considerably less than half of the total one finds in metropolitan Chicago. In what remained largely a country of yeoman farmers until the twentieth century, it is therefore not necessary to have black informants in every community investigated.

The distribution of the population is a peculiar one by the lights of a South Carolinian. Unlike a gentle gradation from counties of smaller to those of larger populations, there are sharp contrasts. With nearly a hundred counties and a state population of 3,600,000, there are many counties under ten thousand; in 1960 Van Buren barely topped 4000. There are four cities—Memphis, Nashville, Chattanooga and Knoxville—well over a hundred thousand, with Memphis vying with New Orleans and Atlanta for leadership in the Southeast; but the fifth city in size, Jackson, is just a little above 30,000. The big four have true metropolitan areas, to be investigated under special plans designed for such areas; elsewhere one may simply follow the usual practice in the Middle and South Atlantic and North-Central States, of considering the county as the community and working out from the county seat.

Public education in Tennessee—as anywhere in the United States—has varied in quality from place to place. As for higher education, in contrast with the prestige of Virginia and North Carolina—especially the latter—the state university, like most of those in the South, began to move toward distinction only with the New Deal, the new affluence of mid-century industrialization in the South, and the example set by Huey Long at L.S.U.[7] In some small communities, such as Sewanee, the company village of the Episcopal province, we have such peculiar but long-established cultural centers that one might well look for local cultivated informants as part of the statewide plan. Beside Sewanee, and perhaps Monteagle, one naturally thinks of Bell Buckle and Maryville as deserving consideration.

The settlement history will need to be analyzed in some detail before a work plan can be established; but we know enough already, from several sources, to have a good idea of the general pattern. Many times in my field work, both in the South and in the Middle West, I have had informants tell me a legend of three brothers among their Ulster Scots forbears who arrived in the New World, landed in Philadelphia, and struck out west. In the classical form of the story, the oldest either stayed in western Pennsylvania or stopped in the Shenandoah Valley; the second went on to take up land in the Carolina Up-Country; the third proceeded to Tennessee or Kentucky, or on to the southern part of the Great Lakes region—and the archetypical figure, Daniel Boone, ended his days in Missouri. For my own clansmen—spelled with a small *c*—there is experiential evidence of the truth of this legend. My friend Fritz Frauchiger, now of the Foreign Service Institute but formerly of the University of Oklahoma, married the daughter of a McDavid from Hillsboro, Illinois; the sect is still flourishing on Hillsboro, as attested by my wife's editorial correspondence for the *Illinois Schools Journal.* Twice in my Middle Western field work—first in 1950, in MacLeansboro, Illinois, later, in 1954, in Whitesburg, Kentucky—I ran across a distant kinsman from Mountain City, Tennessee. Although he was somewhat shorter than most of my South Carolina kin, the eyes, face, head shape, and complexion were so much like my father's that anyone in Greenville, South Carolina, would have recognized him as a McDavid. And oddly enough, one of the first questions he asked me was a familiar one: "Did anybody ever ask you if you were

---

[7] Even in football the University of Tennessee was little renowned before the appointment of the late General Robert Neyland as head coach in the late 1920s.

Jewish?"[8] Finally, on my latest visit to Knoxville I discovered that one of the columnists for the university newspaper was Foy McDavid, almost certainly a son of my first cousin who practices law in Harriman, Tennessee; his grandfather, my Uncle Jim, sold his farm in Greenville County in the 1920s and moved to North Carolina, where the elder Foy McDavid went to law school before resuming the trek to the west.

We can also learn something from the backgrounds of the four presidents who launched their political careers in Tennessee. Andrew Jackson was from York County, South Carolina; his protegé, James K. Polk, was born across the line in Mecklenburg County, North Carolina; Andrew Johnson was from Raleigh, on the edge of the plantation country; as a cracker, illiterate till after his marriage, he was at least as alien as the other two to the amenities of plantation culture and, unlike them, he never acquired the wealth to adapt him to that culture. And Sam Houston, the founder of the Lone Star Republic, who started his political career in Tennessee, was born in Rockbridge County, Virginia, in the Shenandoah Valley. Digging a little deeper, we find that many of the earliest settlers of East Tennessee were unhung alumni of the abortive Regulator insurrection in colonial North Carolina—a frontier protest against the domination of the colony by the plantation interests, and particularly against the absence of accessible courts in which the frontiersmen could seek redress of grievances. It was the same complaint that in Virginia gave rise to the institution of *lynching,* named after one of its founders, though both Judge Lynch and the Regulators observed the tradition of common law and due process, unlike latter-day practitioners, whether white in Mississippi or black in the South Side branches of the Chicago City College. In any event, the preponderance of early settlers in Tennessee were immediately from the South Midland, ultimately from Pennsylvania.

The settlement of eastern Tennessee is documented as proceeding by three routes. The earliest settlements, in the Watauga Valley, followed that river from western North Carolina. Slightly

---

[8] Since in Ireland the patronymic *McDavid* was reputedly assumed by de Burghs and Burkes who took to the bush after trouble with Sassenach law, the question is not without its amusing personal overtones.

later, other settlers came from North Carolina through two other tributary valleys of the Tennessee, the Pigeon and the French Broad. The easiest route—that overland, from the headwaters of the Shenandoah to the headwaters of the Tennessee—was soon opened by the Virginians. And finally, South Carolinians and Georgians came from the upper reaches of the Savannah and its tributaries, around the southern slope of the Smokies. Even in the Smokies, putatively a uniform relic area, all three of these routes are well documented. Once arrived in Tennessee, the settlers used the river systems rather than overland routes; thus Robertson's colony at Nashville was founded by pioneers who rafted down the Tennessee and then back up the Cumberland.

The western part of the state, like that of Kentucky, was the last to be settled, after a special purchase from the Chickasaw Indians. This brought Tennessee into contact with the keel boats, barges, and steamboats along the Mississippi and its tributaries, a cultural situation that has splintered the east-west bundles of isoglosses, even as the Rhine has blurred the dialect boundary between Low and High German. It is unlikely that we will find a belt of North Midland influence, such as we find along the Ohio Valley in Kentucky, but we should not be surprised if we find a few North Midland items brought down from Pittsburgh or occasional forms brought upriver from New Orleans and the Gulf Coast. As to what items we might look for, I refer you to my article in the forthcoming Festschrift for Hans Kurath on the folk vocabulary of eastern Kentucky.[9] But let us discuss a few problems.

In vocabulary, we have the interpenetration of South Midland, general Midland, and local Southern terms. In eastern Kentucky we find almost everywhere the West Virginia *coffee sack* 'burlap bag,' but we also find the Chesapeake Bay *(sea) grass sack* and the North Carolina *tow sack*. In Tennessee we may expect all of these, and as well the South Carolina and Virginia Piedmont *crocus sack* or *croaker sack*. In eastern Kentucky we have prevailingly the Carolina *woods colt* 'bastard,' but also the Virginia *baseborn (child)*. The Southern coastal *carry you home* 'escort' is rare in eastern Kentucky, but is normal in the speech of one of my

---

[9] *The Festschrift*, edited by Harald Scholler and John Reidy, is scheduled for publication at Phillips University, Marburg/Lahn, Germany, in 1971.

Chicago students, a black brought up in Dayton, Tennessee; it is probably to be expected in the eastern part of the state. The mountain *pack* 'to carry'—where South Carolinians would *tote*—was in the 1940s normal usage in Lebanon, now a jitney-jaunt from Nashville; there, too, I first encountered *wardrobe* in the sense of a built-in closet—*clothes-closet*, that is—rather than a piece of furniture, a usage I later found in Scottsville, Kentucky. Perhaps this is characteristic of the Nashville basin.

In pronunciation we might expect to find (at least in the speech of the younger generation), as elsewhere west of the Appalachians, a collapsing of the historical phonemic differences before intervocalic /-r-/, as in *merry, marry, Mary*, or before postvocalic /-r/, as in *hoarse* and *horse*. I would hesitate to predict that some informants, perhaps in the northwestern part of the state, might contrast *hoarse* and *horse* but fail to distinguish *form* from *farm*. Still, this homonymy is so widespread, in the St. Louis area, along the Ohio Valley, and in parts of southwestern Louisiana and east Texas, that I should not be surprised to find it. With poor whites rising to affluence and education, we may well find a spread of postvocalic /-r/; yet in 1939 I found the [3⨯] diphthong, in *bird* and the like, among Alabama undergraduates as far up the Tennessee River as Athens, Alabama. I wonder what has happened since then.

Nor are there lacking unresolved grammatical problems. The American situation is so different from the British that I have found myself unable to elicit many of the critical grammatical forms by direct questioning, let alone by paradigms. Yet I have found in Kentucky (and here I give a commercial for my wife's dissertation)[10] not only the anticipated forms from the South and South Midland, and even eastern Virginia, but certain indigenous uses, such as *brought on* 'not made at home,' and *used to* as a sentence-initial adverb equivalent to 'formerly,' as in "*used to*, everybody around here baked their own bread." And in territory far removed from any serious contact with black speech, I have found widespread evidence of such alleged "Black English" forms as the uninflected third singular present indicative, or the finite *be*.

---

[10]Virginia G. McDavid, "Verb Forms in the North-Central States and Upper Midwest," Diss. U. of Minnesota 1956.

These are but samples of the forces and problems with which the investigator of Tennessee speech will have to reckon. As one who has worked in similar areas, I cannot minimize the difficulties facing the field workers. But if I were under forty, I would leap at the opportunity. I envy those who have it.

SOUTHERN SPEECH AND THE LAGS PROJECT

Lee Pederson

Emory University

§ For all the popular attention Southern speech receives, no other large set of regional and social dialects in this country has been treated less systematically by American linguists than those varieties of English spoken in the cultural area dominated by the Confederate States of America (1861–1865). Virtually unsupported by American structuralists, the Linguistic Atlas of the United States and Canada (LAUSC) Project was unable to get through the interior South, so, despite its excellent coverage of the Virginias, the Carolinas, and large areas of Georgia and Florida, the Deep South—the states of Alabama, Arkansas, Louisiana, Mississippi, Tennessee, and Texas—is uncharted territory in terms of traditional European linguistic geography.[1] It is, therefore, impossible to formulate invulnerable generalizations about the regional speech of the South or to characterize its sociolinguistic complexities, e.g., matters of caste, class, and cultivation in relation to regional dialect patterns. And these have become important goals in general and applied linguistics, where questions of theory evaluation and compensatory education cannot be answered by either the undisciplined expertise of local dilettantes or the conventional wisdom of the mass media.

The following summary of the aims, methods, and preliminary

---

[1]Although many summaries of the LAUSC Project include discussions of its aims and methods, the basic statements of Hans Kurath in the *Handbook of the Linguistic Geography of New England* (Providence, Rhode Island: Brown University Press, 1939) require no modification in 1970. Three essays which summarize ongoing research since 1939 are Raven I. McDavid, Jr.'s "Regional Linguistic Atlases in the United States," *Orbis* 5 (1956), 349–386, and "The Second Round of Dialectology in North American English," *Journal of the Canadian Linguistic Association* 6 (1960), 108–114, and E. Bagby Atwood's "The Methods of American Dialectology," *Zeitschrift für Mundartsforschung* 30 (1963), 1–30.

research of the Linguistic Atlas of the Gulf States (LAGS) Project concerns only the immediate backgrounds of that work and defers its theoretical and practical applications to specialists in those activities. Although a logical extension of the LAUSC Project, the regional impetus for the LAGS Project is conveniently marked by an oral symposium at Duke University, February 10-11, 1966, sponsored by the University Center for Southern Studies in the Social Sciences and the Humanities. Several useful programmatic essays were read there, but two statements are directly related to current research plans. These are the remarks of Raven I. McDavid, Jr., and J. Kenneth Moreland.

In his overview, "Needed Research in Southern Dialects," McDavid acknowledged the work already completed, established a set of priorities for dialect study in the South, and explained the use of this work in terms of science and education. Observing the problem from several perspectives—as the editor of the *Linguistic Atlas of the Middle and South Atlantic States*, as an experienced Atlas fieldworker, as a coordinator of several urban language projects in Chicago, as an English teacher, and as a native Southerner—he recognized the need not only for a completion of the first round survey to complement work done to the north and west but also for a careful investigation of relic areas (such as Appalachia) from which the rural Southerners emerge and focal areas (such as Atlanta and Memphis) to which these same immigrants are drawn. When such research problems are under control and a baseline has been identified, a wider range of investigation will be possible for students of Southern speech and general linguistics, e.g., the intricacies of Gullah, Louisiana Black-French, Florida and Texas Spanish-American English, as well as the speech of such disparate Southern bilinguals as the Germans, Czechs, and Cherokees.[2]

As a cultural anthropologist who has closely watched the post-World War II developments in the South, J. Kenneth Moreland in "Anthropology and the Study of Culture, Society, and Community in the South" added a note of urgency to the complicated research program outlined by McDavid:

---

[2] In *Perspectives on the South: Agenda for Research,* Edgar T. Thompson, ed. (Durham, N.C.: Duke University Press, 1967), 111-120.

The South might be characterized as a formerly distinctive region that is fast losing its distinctiveness. It has been different from other American regions in its caste-like system of race relations, its agriculturally based economy and its relatively slow industrialization and urbanization, its fundamentalistic religion, and its feeling of separateness from the rest of the nation. All of these characteristics are probably being altered as cultural traits and patterns throughout America become similar.[3]

As Moreland encouraged anthropologists to witness a culture in transition and to record its characteristics before they are beyond recognition, he isolated a central concern of the linguistic geographers in the South who must investigate the local dialects—record, analyze, and describe them—before they are completely assimilated by the process of cultural evolution.

As an extension of the LAUSC Project by affiliation, the LAGS Project uses the empirical method developed by Hans Kurath and his associates over the past 40 years.[4] This survey of Southern speech is intended to cover evenly the Gulf States of Florida, Alabama, Mississippi, Louisiana, and Texas, as well as the neighboring states of Georgia, Tennessee, and Arkansas. From the preliminary research begun in 1967 to the present (February, 1970), the organization of this project has been developed through bibliographical and field investigations, conferences, and data analysis which have determined the aims and methods of the work to be done.

With the aid and encouragement of James B. McMillan, who has collected and described the linguistic scholarship of Southern speech for more than 30 years, a review of source material was begun in the summer of 1967. The region comprised in that survey included those states generally recognized as *Southern* by American social scientists: the 11 members of the Confederacy, Oklahoma and West Virginia, which were organized as political enti-

---

[3]*Ibid.*, 140.
[4]Besides the titles in note 1, see Hans Kurath, *A Word Geography of the Eastern United States* (Ann Arbor: University of Michigan Press, 1949); E. Bagby Atwood, *A Survey of Verb Forms in the Eastern United States* (Ann Arbor: University of Michigan Press, 1953); Hans Kurath and Raven I. McDavid, Jr., *The Pronunciation of English in the Atlantic States* (Ann Arbor: University of Michigan Press, 1961); Hans Kurath, *A Phonology and Prosody of Modern English* (Ann Arbor: University of Michigan Press, 1964).

ties after the Civil War, and the border states of Kentucky and Missouri.[5]

The bibliographical survey was summarized under three headings: 1) *Bibliography,* current and completed indices, 2) *Structural Descriptions,* overviews and more specialized—regional, subregional, and local—accounts of phonological, morphological, and syntactic problems, and 3) *Cultural Interpretations,* sociological and philological analyses of native Southern speech.[6] Although very few discoveries were made that are not common knowledge to all serious students of Southern speech, the review did bring several aspects of the subject into perspective for the LAGS Project:

> *first,* that Southern speech is not a single regional dialect, but, rather, a complicated set of at least eight clearly marked patterns, from which at least 11 derivative regional dialects are developed and which extend from Northeast Kentucky to Southwest Texas;[7]
>
> *next,* that several critical features of Southern phonology were closely studied long before American structuralism became operational in the 1940s;[8]

---

[5] E.g., William A. Read in "The Vowel System of the Southern United States," *Englische Studien* 41 (1910), W. T. Couch, ed., in *Culture in the South* (Chapel Hill: University of North Carolina Press, 1934), and Edgar T. Thompson, *op. cit.* (1967).

[6] Lee Pederson, *An Annotated Bibliography of Southern Speech,* Southeastern Education Laboratory Monograph 1 (Atlanta, 1968).

[7] McDavid (1956), 349–386.

[8] E.g., on nasalized vowels and their phonemic status, see Read (1910), James B. McMillan, "Vowel Nasality as a Sandhi-form of the Morphemes *-nt* and *-ing* in Southern American," *American Speech* 14 (1939), 120–123, James B. McMillan, "A Phonology of the Standard English of East Central Alabama," Diss. University of Chicago 1946, Chapters 2, 3, and 5, and T. E. Johnson, "Nasality in Southern Speech," *Southern Speech Journal,* 17 (1951), 30–35; on postvocalic *r,* see William A. Read, "The Southern *r,*" *Louisiana School Review* 17 (1910), 235–245, (or, more conveniently, *Louisiana State University Bulletin* 1 (1910); on the vowel phoneme (/ai/) and its phonic details, see Harry S. Wise, "A Phonetic Study of the Southern American 'ai'," Thesis Louisiana State University 1937; on consonants other than *r,* see William A. Read, "Some Variant Pronunciations in the New South," *Dialect Notes* 3 (1911), 496–536, Nathaniel M. Caffee, "Southern 'l' Plus a Consonant," *American Speech* 15 (1940), 259–261, and Nathaniel M. Caffee, "Some Notes on Consonant Pronunciation in the South," *Studies for William A. Read,* ed. N. M. Caffee and T. A. Kirby, (Baton Rouge: Louisiana State University Press, 1940), 125–132, and McMillan (1946); on intonation, see Read (1911).

furthermore, that sociolinguistic investigation of Southern speech includes pioneer work in both the identification of caste and class by phonetic and phonemic markers and the recognition of caste by vocal quality;[9]

finally, that with few exceptions, descriptions of Southern speech have been written from the standpoint of the White caste to the exclusion of the Black caste.[10]

Those observations were useful in planning the Dialect Survey of Rural Georgia,[11] a preliminary investigation for the LAGS Project of selected phonological, grammatical, and lexical features in a network of rural communities (i.e., with populations under 2,500 in 1960) in 30-mile grids across the state. Its immediate aims are to improve present understanding of the regional dialect boundaries in Georgia, to provide more nearly precise statements about caste distinctions separating Black and White speech, as well as between the speech of the "insiders," who are often called "Town Whites," and the "outsiders," who are regularly called

---

[9] The first sociolinguistic investigation based on the systematically contrastive data of the LAUSC Project was Raven I. McDavid, Jr., "Postvocalic *r* in South Carolina: A Social Analysis," *American Speech* 23 (1948), 194–203; the first controlled investigation of social identification by speech characteristics was Milton Dickens and Granville M. Sawyer, "An Experimental Comparison of Vocal Quality among Mixed Groups of Whites and Negroes," *Southern Speech Journal* 17 (1952), 178–185.

[10] A few exceptions include Lorenzo D. Turner, *Africanisms in the Gullah Dialect* (Chicago: University of Chicago Press, 1949), Raven I. McDavid, Jr., and Virginia G. McDavid, "The Relationship of the Speech of American Negroes to the Speech of Whites," *American Speech* 26 (1951), 3–17, Saunders Walker, "A Dictionary of Folk Speech of the East Alabama Negro," Diss. Western Reserve University 1956, and Juanita V. Williamson, "A Phonological and Morphological Study of the Speech of Negroes of Memphis, Tennessee," Diss. University of Michigan 1961. Perhaps the most perceptive essay ever written on the subject of Black speech is C. M. Wise, "Negro Dialect," *Quarterly Journal of Speech* 19 (1933), 522–528, where such complicated matters as paralanguage and influence of the Black caste are discussed informally.

[11] Supported by the Emory University Research Committee and the Linguistic Research and Demonstration Center for the Rome City Schools, Rome, Georgia, the Dialect Survey of Rural Georgia investigates the speech of natives over age 65, a better and lesser educated pair of Blacks and Whites. A questionnaire of approximately 300 items is based on LAUSC worksheets for the South Atlantic States and the instrument described by E. Bagby Atwood, *The Regional Vocabulary of Texas* (Austin: University of Texas Press, 1962), 30–35. More than 200 interviews have been completed at this time, and the remaining 100 should be done by June, 1970.

"Poor Whites," and to find potentially significant linguistic forms which serve as regional or social markers and which might be added to the worksheets of the LAGS Project.

By July, 1969, 100 records from 25 communities had been transcribed and organized for analysis with phonetic, phonemic, and morphological description, from which several generalizations concerning regional and social patterns in rural Northern Georgia were drawn.[12] These included nine patterns of regional and social distribution as they relate to the South Midland-Upcountry Lower Southern dialect boundary. On the basis of fieldwork conducted by Guy Lowman in the 1940s and by Raven I. McDavid, Jr., in the 1940s and 1950s, McDavid projected the boundary out of South Carolina, where it had been well established by extensive fieldwork, into Georgia, where the investigation had been less intensive.[13] McDavid's extrapolations and the preliminary findings of the Georgia Survey are included in Map 2: line A marks the probable southern extent of the South Midland area and line B marks the probable northern extent of the Upcountry Lower Southern area, which are McDavid's extrapolations; line C reflects the current rural survey and its interpretation of topographical, cultural, and linguistic data.

The basis for the nine patterns identified in the rural survey are three phonetic markers [a∼a.] of /ai/ in *white, write,* or *rice* (i.e., before voiceless stops and fricatives), [oə] of /o/ in *road,* and [3Ŧ] of /r/ or /3/ or /ðr/ (depending on the phonemic interpretation) in *bird, dirt, purse, hers, worm,* or *girl,* two phonemic markers, /r/ in *horse,* and /d/ in *the* (under weak stress at the outset of a noun phrase), one syntactic marker, the absence of a linking verb, the so-called "zero copula," as in *he dead* for *he is dead,* and three lexical markers, *French harp* for *harmonica, mouth harp, mouth organ,* or *harp, lightwood* (usually with five phonemes /laitŦd/) for *pine, fat pine, richwood, splinters,* or *fat wood* and *croaker sack, crocus sack,* or *crocus bag* for *tow sack, sack, burlap bag, cloth sack, guano sack, burlap sack, cloth bag, feed bag, sacking, gunny sack, feed sack, claw sack, chicken feed sack, bagging sack, jute sack, corn sack, clothes sack,* or *bag.*

---

[12] Lee Pederson, "Dialect Patterns in Rural Northern Georgia," in press.

[13] McDavid (1956), Map 2, "Tentative Dialect Boundaries," 355.

These nine features, all of which are conventional regional or social markers in American dialect study, showed a generally predictable pattern of regional distribution. The phonetic forms [oᵊ] and [3ɨ], the phonemic incidence of /d/, the syntactic "zero copula," and the lexical items *lightwood* and *croaker sack,* etc., prevailed in the Upcountry Lower Southern area, and the monophthongs of /ai/, the presence of /r/ in *horse,* and the preference of *French harp* prevailed in the South Midland area. These basic patterns of distribution were, however, disturbed by the recessive patterns which were, for the most part, restricted to the speech of poor Blacks and Whites who do not participate in the affairs of the dominant culture. Poor Blacks, as far north as the Blue Ridge Mountains in Helen (A4) in White County, preserve many relics of Upcountry Lower Southern speech, and "Poor Whites," as far south as Lincolnton (C7) along the Savannah River in Lincoln County and Warrenton (D6) in Warren County in the heart of the heaviest concentration of Black population in rural Northern Georgia, maintain forms which are standard markers of South Midland speech.

A further analysis of the North Georgia data has concentrated on the obstruent system, the 16 classes of consonant phonemes which include /p/b/t/d/k/g/f/v/ə/ð /s/z/š/ž/.[14] Four tentative conclusions of that discussion are these:

> 1. The obstruent system in rural Northern Georgia is highly complicated by several recurrent features which usually involve phonotactic patterning and which invariably result in a higher incidence of phonemic alternation in these environments—often involving specific processes of assimilation—and phonemic loss than are found in other observed dialects of American English.
>
> 2. The incidence of these recessive features is considerably higher among Upcountry Lower Southerners than among South Midland speakers. At least two of these features, however, have been conventionalized and are widespread throughout the territory of Northern Georgia, the products of medial and final devoicing of stop consonants in *spigot* /g/>/k/ and in *salad* /d/>/t/; actually *salit ~ salət* is standard in British dialects (Wright EDG, § 305) and is attested from the 14th C (OED).

---

[14] Lee Pederson, "English Obstruents in Rural Northern Georgia," in press.

3. Overall, but especially in the Upcountry Lower Southern area, the highest incidence of these recessive features is recorded among Blacks, and those Whites with the greatest number of these recessive forms in their speech live where the Black population is most heavily concentrated—everywhere south of the Chattahoochee River, but most notably in close proximity of Atlanta in the southeast quadrant of the area and along the Savannah River in the southeast.

4. Some of the most complicated problems of phonemic classification within the obstruent system in rural Northern Georgia involve forms with grammatical functions. The alveolar stops /t/d/ are regular preterit signals among the reflexes of the Old English weak verbs; the alveolar fricatives /s/z/ mark tense and number in all verb paradigms, and these same fricatives indicate number and possession in the case system which accommodates most English nouns. Although these phono-syntactic problems are beyond the range of a phonemic outline, the implications seem inescapable: unless a grammar of American English is carefully limited to a description of "General American" (that fictional dialect spoken by no one), syntactic analysis requires a much more sensitive phonological interpretation than is currently available from either generative or unregenerate structuralists and future dialect surveys of American English require close attention to the pronunciation of consonants, as well as the vowels, and to the distribution of linguistic forms among the Blacks, as well as the Whites.

Another important source of information for planners of the LAGS Project was a conference of 10 linguistic geographers in Atlanta, May 16–17, 1968, who met to organize the program.[15] In addition to recommendations concerning a real delimitation and the training of fieldworkers, these points were made:

> The Atlas questionnaire should be modified as radically as necessary to meet the needs of the Project in developing the LAGS worksheets, but its form should be kept as a frame of reference to preserve as much of its productive content as possible toward the collection of systematically contrastive data

---

[15] With the assistance of W. Gene Watson, former research coordinator for Southeastern Education Laboratory and now director of the Nueva Day School, Menlo Park, California, these participants included: Harold B. Allen (University of Minnesota), Hans Kurath (University of Michigan), Raven I. McDavid, Jr. (University of Chicago), James B. McMillan (University of Alabama), Lee Pederson (Emory University), William R. Van Riper (Louisiana State University), R. Hood Roberts (Center for Applied Linguistics), Rudolph Troike (University of Texas), Juanita V. Williamson (LeMoyne College), and Gordon R. Wood (Southern Illinois University at Edwardsville).

for comparison with material collected by LAUSC fieldworkers in neighboring states, as well as within the Gulf States territory, viz., in Florida and Georgia.

The selection of communities must include attention to both regional coverage (i.e., an even survey of the territory) and social characteristics (i.e., a representation of community types, e.g., rural, urban, suburban). This is especially important in establishing a baseline for sociolinguistic research in urban centers, Atlanta, Birmingham, Dallas, Memphis, Nashville, and New Orleans.

The selection of informants should be done as systematically as possible, i.e., insofar as a realistic application of judgment sampling procedure permits a flexible program of basic inventorial field research.

Those recommendations were central considerations in the organization of the first phase of the LAGS fieldwork, which is intended to provide a skeletal outline of the regional dialects and which will be followed by further research determined by those initial findings. At this point, plans include the organization of the worksheets, the identification of target communities, and the selection of informants in those places.

The LAUSC worksheets for the Middle and South Atlantic States are the basic text for the LAGS investigation. These include more than 800 items of phonology, morphology, syntax, and vocabulary, both a common core which is shared by all other forms of LAUSC worksheets and a special set of items which is derived from preliminary research and informal observation. The main source of addenda is the Dialect Survey of Rural Georgia, but McDavid's research in Kentucky, Van Riper's Oklahoma survey, Atwood's Texas survey, and several other sources have also been useful. Four basic kinds of additions have been made: *phonological items,* especially words and phrases which provide contexts for consonants in all syllabic positions; *morphological items,* especially forms which reflect grammatical and morphophonemic operations; *conversation topics* to establish situations in which free and controlled discussion might provide data for preliminary analysis of intonation, paralanguage, and stylistic variation; *lexical items* with tentative regional or social significance, especially those forms which seem to suggest settlement patterning.

The identification of communities is based on an analysis of urban and rural places in Alabama, where the first LAGS interviews were made. Six basic types of communities are isolated there on the basis of population and social characteristics. In 1965, the population of Alabama was estimated at 3,500,000 with 55% of that total classified as urban and 45% as rural. The following set of community types include:

1. *Birmingham Type Communities* (BTC) are urban centers, large and influential metropolitan areas with populations in excess of 100,000: Birmingham (340,000), Mobile (203,000), and Montgomery (135,000);

2. *Huntsville Type Communities* (HTC) are rapidly expanding centers of culture with populations in excess of 50,000: Huntsville (73,000), Tuscaloosa (64,000), and Gadsden (58,000);

3. *Pritchard Type Communities* (PTC) are large towns and smaller dormitory suburbs which are within spheres of urban influence, e.g.: Pritchard (48,000) and Chickasaw (10,000) near Mobile; Homewood (20,000), Fairfield (16,000), and Mountain Brook (13,000) near Birmingham;

4. *Florence Type Communities* (FTC) are a mixed set of expanding, stable, and declining towns, smaller than HTC and distinguished from the urban-dominated PTC, with populations in excess of 25,000: Florence (35,000), Anniston (35,000), Bessemer (33,000), Decatur (31,000), Dothan (31,000), and Selma (28,000);

5. *Opelika Type Communities* (OTC) are a mixed set of expanding, stable, and declining towns, smaller than FTC and distinguished from the urban-dominated PTC, with populations in excess of 10,000: Opelika (16,000), Talladega (18,000), Auburn (16,000), Alexander City (13,000), Sheffield (14,000), Analusia (11,000), Cullman (11,000), Enterprise (11,000), Jasper (11,000), Ozark (10,000), and Troy (10,000);

6. *Arab Type Communities* (ATC) are a mixed set of expanding, stable, but usually declining rural places with populations under 10,000, e.g., Arab (3,000), Jackson (5,000), Haleyville (4,000), Abbeville (3,000), Brewton (6,000), Clanton (6,000), and Tuskegee (2,000).

In addition to those 35 places, where interviews have been or will be soon completed, several other communities will be selected in Alabama later, but, for now, these characterizations include all places in the state except Phoenix City, that unique rest and relaxation center for the military personnel of Fort Benning, Georgia, across the river near Columbus.

The selection of informants will certainly reflect social characteristics of the communities, but this will involve a survey of potential social dialects rather than an equational representation of population statistics. The basic LAUSC classification of folk (Type I), common (Type II), and cultivated (Type III) speakers is used, and three primary social groups—Blacks, "Poor Whites," and "Town Whites"—are presently identified. Further distinctions, e.g., age, occupation, marital status, religion, sex, and, possibly, social integration (viz., LAUSC A&B distinctions), will be useful in the analysis of the data, but it remains undecided at this time whether these characteristics will be used in the direct selection of informants beyond the usual LAUSC method of representing as many social types as possible. During the first phase of the investigation, emphasis will be placed upon the selection of older informants (over age 35) among the three primary types (I, II, III) and the three social groups (Black, "Poor White," and "Town White").

The format of the worksheets will not be determined until all areas of the LAGS territory have been surveyed in a preliminary way. It is also impossible to outline all of the communities at this time or to predict the number of field records which will be collected during the course of the project. Since the region is quite large and socially complicated, however, it seems reasonable to expect a basic corpus in excess of 1,000 records to represent the Gulf States territory in a culturally sensitive and historically reflective wide-mesh survey.

Participants in the LAGS Project currently include:

Directors: Raven I. McDavid, Jr. (Consultant) and Lee Pederson (Field)

General Consultants: Harold B. Allen, James B. McMillan, R. Hood Roberts, Rudolph Troike, William R. Van Riper, Juanita V. Williamson, and Gordon R. Wood

Executive Secretary: Lorraine H. Burghardt

Fieldworkers: C. William Foster (Alabama, Mississippi, and Western Tennessee), Lorraine H. Burghardt (Eastern Tennessee), Patricia Lowery (Middle Georgia and Alabama), Lee Pederson (Alabama, Georgia, and Mississippi), and Ursala Walker (Florida).

Map 1: The Lags Territory

142   Dialectology: Problems and Perspectives

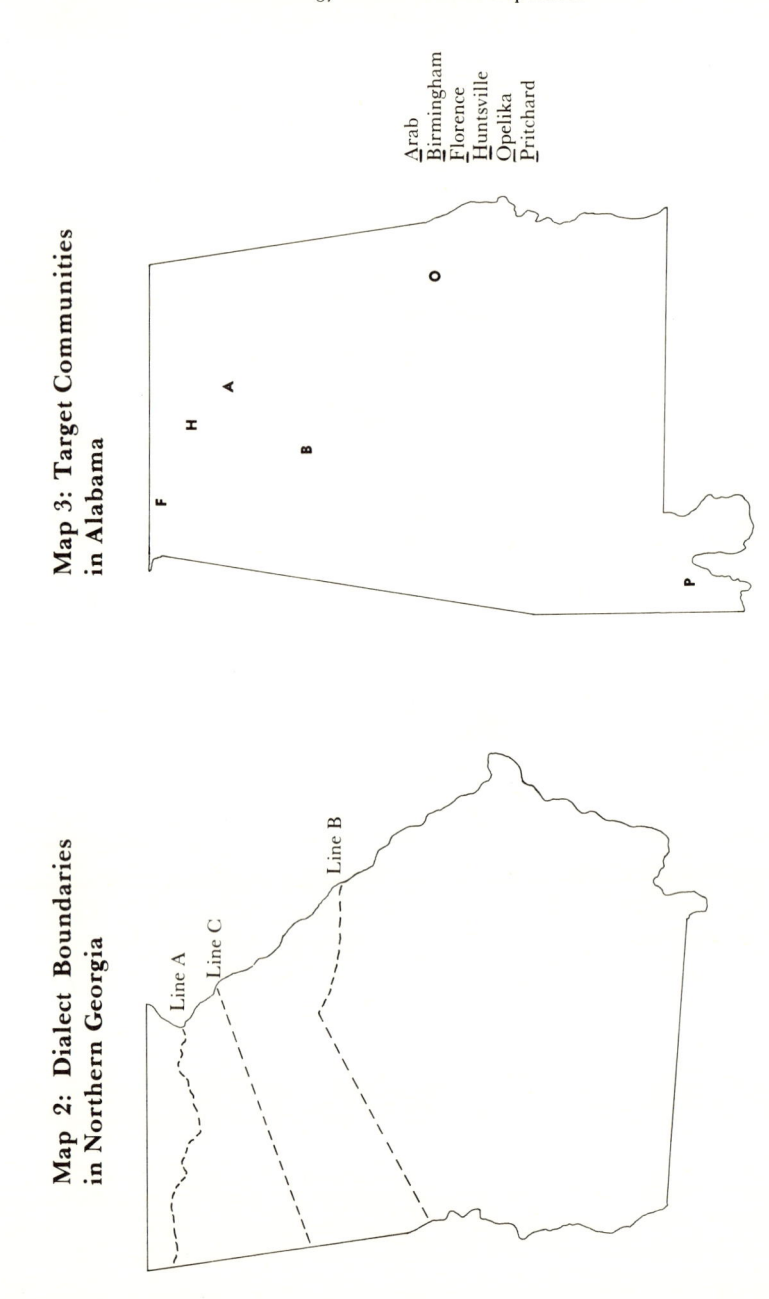

Arab
Birmingham
Florence
Huntsville
Opelika
Pritchard

Map 3: Target Communities in Alabama

Map 2: Dialect Boundaries in Northern Georgia

Line A
Line C
Line B

BELMONT COLLEGE LIBRARY